GOOGLE ADS STRATEGIES

A COMPLETE GUIDE

KORAY ODABASI

Copyright © Koray Odabasi

All rights reserved.

First Edition   : October 2020

No part of this publication may be reproduced in any form, or by any means (electronic, mechanical, photocopying, recording, or otherwise), or any information browsing, storage, or retrieval system, without permission in writing from the publisher.

Requests for permission should be directed to koray@korayodabasi.com

For the latest information, visit korayodabasi.com

GOOGLE ADS STRATEGIES

A COMPLETE GUIDE

DISCOVER UP TO DATE AND EFFECTIVE STRATEGIES

ACHIEVE MAXIMUM CONVERSION

TABLE OF CONTENTS

1. UNDERSTANDING THE WEB & THE USERS   11

- Today's Consumers See Hundreds of Messages Every Day (Other Than Your Ad)
- Mobile Performance is Critical for Success
- You Should Charm the Users in a Few Seconds

2. THE TRUTH IS NO ONE WANTS TO SEE ADS   17

- It Is Your Money. If You Want to Throw Good Money after Bad, It Is Your Choice
- Communicate the Right Message, to the Right Person, at the Right Time

3. GOOGLE ADS PROJECT   23

- Google Search Ads vs. SEO
- What to Expect from Google Ads Campaigns?
- What Is the Value of Google Ads Campaigns?
- How Can You Monitor the Results?
- Which KPI's Should You Follow?

4. SCOPE OF GOOGLE ADS PROJECT   37

- Which Products / Categories Should You Target?
- Targeting Products and Services

5. SEGMENT YOUR AUDIENCE 43

- Demographic Segmentation: Who Is Your Target Audience?
- Psychographic Segmentation: What Kind of Personality Does Your Target Audience Have?
- Geographical Segmentation: Where Will You Reach Your Target Audience?
- Behavioral Segmentation: What Motivates Your Target Audience to Buy?

6. LANDING PAGES AND CONVERSION 51

7. SETTING CAMPAIGNS AND AD GROUPS 59

- What Should Be the Campaign Structure?
- How Should You Organize the Ad Groups?

8. MAIN COMPONENTS OF GOOGLE ADS CAMPAIGNS 65

- Location
- Demographics
- Devices, Operating Systems and Networks
- Language
- Ad Schedule
- Budget
- Bidding
- Audiences
- Audience Targeting

9. GOOGLE SEARCH ADS 99

- Networks
- Keyword Matching Options
- Free SEO Sites and Tools for Keyword Research
- Which Keywords Should You Use?

- Tips to Refine the Keywords
- Effective Tips for Negative Keywords List
- What Determines the Quality Score? How Can You Get the Highest Quality Score?
- How Can You Write the Ad Content Effectively?
- How Can You Use the Ad Extensions Effectively?
- Using Audiences in Search Ads
- How Can You Benefit from Auction Insights?
- Branded Campaign Strategies
- Product (& Service) Campaign Strategies
- Dynamic Search Ads

10. GOOGLE DISPLAY ADS   151

- Remarketing Ads
- Display Ads

11. SHOPPING ADS   163

- Google Merchant Center
- Shopping Ads
- Smart Shopping Ads
- Dynamic Remarketing Ads

12. OTHER GOOGLE AD TYPES   173

- Gmail Ads
- YouTube Ads
- Local Search Ads

13. TIPS TO IMPROVE CAMPAIGN PERFORMANCE   183

- Case 1: Your daily budget is running out too fast
- Case 2: Your conversion is too low
- Case 3: You want to reach new audiences

- Case 4: You want to reach global audiences

14. GOOGLE ADS CHECKLIST   189
15. IT IS YOUR TURN   191

WELCOME

We live in a world that is noisier than ever.

Today's consumers see hundreds of marketing messages on an average day and recall almost none of them.

Generic marketing messages do not produce results and increasing the budget does not solve this inefficiency.

Segmenting your audience and communicating with each segment using tailored messages is the key to get the attention of the users in 2020.

This approach increases the conversion significantly and generates impressive results even with small budgets.

As a professional who has been working in the field of digital marketing for more than 20 years, I will share special tactics to achieve the best performance in your Google Ads campaigns.

To help you get results, I will provide 30-item checklist at the end of the book.

Many brands implemented these strategies and achieved success.

I am sure that it will be useful to you as well.

Are you ready?

Let's begin.

UNDERSTANDING THE WEB & THE USERS IN 2020

Today's Consumers See Hundreds of Messages Every Day (Other Than Your Ad)

Today's consumers see hundreds of marketing messages on an average day and recall almost none of them.

According to an article published on the American Marketing Association (AMA) website, an average consumer sees 10,000 marketing messages (including product labels) per day.[1]

A study conducted by Microsoft states that consumers are exposed to 600 messages per day.[2]

An article on New York Times states that a person living in a city sees up to 5,000 ad messages per day, based on a research. About half of the people think that marketing and advertising today is out of control.[3]

An article on The Guardian states that in an entire day, we are likely to see 3,500 marketing messages. In an experiment, in 90 minutes, a person saw 250 adverts from more than 100 brands

---

[1] https://www.ama.org/partners/content/Pages/why-customers-attention-scarcest-resources-2017.aspx
[2] http://www.bandt.com.au/marketing/consumers-exposed-600-messages-day-getting-search-right-rules-marketers
[3] https://www.nytimes.com/2007/01/15/business/media/15everywhere.html

in 70 different formats. The number recalled without prompting was only 1. [4]

Every day, users post 95 million photos on Instagram, post 500 million tweets on Twitter, upload more than 700,000 hours of video on YouTube, send 281 billion emails.

The human brain is loaded with 34 gb. of information per day.

Through mobile phones, online services, internet, email, television, radio, newspapers, books, social media, people receive every day about 105,000 words during awake hours.[5]

It is no surprise that people are overwhelmed by these messages and they are trying to find a solution.

As they are bombarded with this huge load of information every day, interest in videos related to "relaxing" is rising, with watch time increasing over 70% in a year.[6]

The ratio of people who are trying to limit smartphone usage increased from 47% in 2017 to 63% in 2018. [7]

People are trying to get rid of ads by ad block software and even if they do not use such software, the attention span has declined to only a few seconds.

The web is noisier than ever, and it is hard to get the attention of the users by generic marketing messages.

Each day bloggers post millions of posts, huge amount of new content is created on the web. However, according to some sources, on average, 80% of readers never make it past the headline.[8]

---

[4] https://www.theguardian.com/media/2005/nov/19/advertising.marketingandpr
[5] https://www.tech21century.com/the-human-brain-is-loaded-daily-with-34-gb-of-information/
[6] https://www.thinkwithgoogle.com/consumer-insights/september-youtube-video-trends/
[7] https://www.bondcap.com/report/itr19/#view/1
[8] https://moz.com/blog/5-data-insights-into-the-headlines-readers-click

These studies contribute to the fact that you need to give priority to fast and tailored communication in your Google Ads campaigns in order to achieve success.

The number of messages people receive has increased so much that people are not reading anymore. They are glancing over content until they see something that they are really interested in.

For this reason, your messages in the Google ads campaigns should match the perspective of the recipients to gain their attention.

Mobile Performance is Critical for Success

Today's digital world is increasingly being shaped by mobile and you should focus on this.

Mobile usage was 0.8 hours in 2011 and increased to 3.6 hours in 2018. [9]

Mobile surpassed TV as the medium attracting the most minutes in the US in 2019.[10]

It is no surprise that the share of mobile devices in total website visits often exceeds 60%.

This means that you should focus on mobile performance in your Google Ads project.

Although the conversion rate is often higher on desktop devices, an increase in the mobile conversion will create significant effect that will boost your results.

---

[9] https://www.bondcap.com/report/itr19/#view/1
[10] https://www.emarketer.com/content/mobile-time-spent-2018

You Should Charm the Users in a Few Seconds

Internet users are distracted, they have short attention spans.

A person checks his/her mobile phone an average of 47 times a day. This number increases to 86 times for young people. 9 out of 10 people check their mobile phones within an hour after they wake up in the morning.[11]

In these micro moments, they are usually glancing over content. They are not interested in messages that do not match their perspective.

In a study conducted by Microsoft with 2,000 participants, it is stated that the attention span of the users declined to only 8 seconds.[12]

Facebook says that people spend on average 1.7 seconds with any given piece of content on mobile.[13]

A research based on 2 billion visits found that 55% of the web users spent fewer than 15 seconds actively on a page.[14]

Note that I am talking about getting the attention of overwhelmed and distracted users. Once you get their attention, naturally you will have more time to communicate with them.

Tailored and to the point communication is the key to grab the attention of these people.

You also need to be fast. These people are impatient and demanding.

90% of consumers wait for an immediate response (within 30 minutes) regarding a support question. This figure is 82% for sales and marketing questions.[15]

---

[11] https://www.emarketer.com/Article/Obsessed-Much-Mobile-Addiction-Real/1016759
[12] http://time.com/3858309/attention-spans-goldfish/
[13] https://fbinsights.files.wordpress.com/2017/03/fbiq_why_creativity_matters.pdf
[14] https://time.com/12933/what-you-think-you-know-about-the-web-is-wrong/

53% of the mobile website visitors leave a page that takes longer than three seconds to load. As the page load time goes from 1 second to 5 seconds, the probability of bounce increases to 90% which significantly deteriorates the conversion in your digital marketing campaigns.[16]

In the previous section, I told you that internet users see hundreds of marketing messages every day, they are glancing over content, and you should match their perspective.

Now, I am telling you that you should communicate with them in a short period of time, using tailored messages.

Although these people are using internet heavily, they are distracted, and you have only a few seconds to charm them.

You cannot achieve this by communicating generic messages with large audiences in your Google Ads campaigns. It will not be enough to get their attention.

You should segment your target audience and provide tailored messages to each segment.

---

[15] https://blog.hubspot.com/news-trends/customer-acquisition-study
[16] https://www.thinkwithgoogle.com/marketing-resources/data-measurement/mobile-page-speed-new-industry-benchmarks/

THE TRUTH IS NO ONE WANTS TO SEE ADS

It Is Your Money. If You Want to Throw Good Money after Bad, It Is Your Choice.

Digital advertising platforms usually yield far more effective results than other advertising channels with their effective segmentation and targeting options.

You can easily measure the performance of your ads and revise them whenever you want.

The key to success in digital advertising campaigns is quite clear: give the right message, to the right person, at the right time.

To achieve this, you should break down your target audience and communicate with each segment using a message that will motivate them the most. You cannot achieve success by using undifferentiated messages presented to everyone.

Most of the companies think that their products and services are great, and consumers will buy them immediately if they hear about them only once.

Rather than focusing on the efficiency of the tailored messages, company executives generally think like "let the large group of people see us now, maybe they will buy our products in the future".

More than one billion websites acting with this perspective try to promote their products and services to the internet users without much care.

What result do they get?

- Over 600 million Ad Block users
- Banner click rates below 0.1%
- Many mobile ad clicks are accidental
- The proportion of users who often click on a mobile ad intentionally is 8%

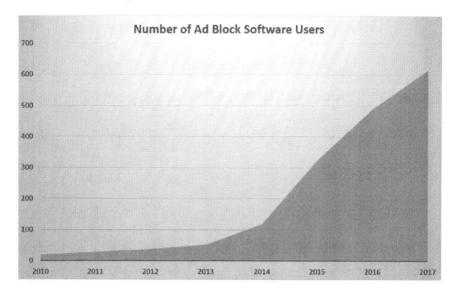

If you do not communicate the right message, to the right person, at the right time, you can easily face the same situation.

83%
I would ban all the mobile ads if I could

According to a research presented on HubSpot, 73% of the participants stated that they dislike pop-up ads and 70% stated that they dislike mobile ads.

The rate of those who stated that online ads are more disturbing than 2-3 years ago reached 91% and the rate of those who stated that they would ban all the mobile ads if they could, reached 83%.[17]

Company executives often tend to maintain their old habits because they do not have sufficient knowledge about the digital environment.

Instead of implementing a detailed plan to reach the target audience effectively, they can spend a large budget to publish short-term banner ads on portals or news sites visited by millions of people having very different profiles (because they think this is more prestigious).

Then, they complain: "I believed in the digital environment and spent so much money, but I did not achieve a significant result.

Media planning agencies usually do not bother to change this perception. This ad model also enables them to earn easy money.

In his talk at Online Marketing Rockstars, Gary Vaynerchuk told that once he was checking a popular news site at short intervals from his mobile phone to follow an important story.

Every time he tried to enter the site, he had to close a banner ad that covered the entire page. As he was trying to reach that website 20 times that day, he accidentally clicked that banner ad 8 times.

The publisher site, the brand, and the digital agency probably thought how great this high click through rate was, but what actually happened was a very bad experience.

He tweeted this experience, posted it on Instagram, and talks about it at conferences mentioning the brand's name.[18]

---

[17] https://research.hubspot.com/why-people-block-ads-and-what-it-means-for-marketers-and-advertisers
[18] https://www.youtube.com/watch?v=eu7z6U8Jdok

Communicate the Right Message, to the Right Person, at the Right Time

More than 1.3 billion websites are competing for visitors.

Most of the brands think that their products or services are great, and they will be sold immediately if they can reach their audience only once.

With this thought, they usually communicate a single marketing message to millions of consumers having different characteristics. They do not differentiate their messages when communicating with different segments.

As a result, the people they are trying to reach, seek for ways to block these messages.

In early 2017, the number of ad blocker software users increased to 230 million on desktop computers and to 380 million on mobile devices.[19]

AdBlock and AdBlock Plus alone had 90 million active users in early 2016.[20]

A research on Statista pointed out that 25.8% of internet users in the US were blocking advertising on their connected devices in 2019.[21]

This is an important challenge for digital marketers, but there is something worse.

Even if the internet users do not use ad blocker software, many of the mobile ad clicks are accidental.

A survey found out that 59% to 73% of consumers say they rarely or never mean to click on ads on their phones.

---

[19] https://www.nytimes.com/2017/01/31/technology/ad-blocking-internet.html
https://pagefair.com/downloads/2017/01/PageFair-2017-Adblock-Report.pdf
[20] https://venturebeat.com/2016/01/22/10-years-in-adblock-plus-passes-500-million-downloads/
[21] https://www.statista.com/statistics/804008/ad-blocking-reach-usage-us/

The rate of the people who often click on a mobile ad intentionally remains only at 4% to 10%.[22]

This is one of the reasons why you hear the word "inbound" so much. The effectiveness of the traditional ad models pushing customers to perform an action decreases day by day.

Do you think that the problem is the ad model itself, or is it irrelevant, generic marketing messages communicated with large audiences?

93% of the people say they receive marketing messages that are not relevant, 90% say irrelevant messages are annoying. 44% of people even think to switch to brands who better personalize marketing messages.[23]

You are trying to convince impatient people who see hundreds of messages every day. You can only achieve this by communicating the right message, to the right person, at the right time.

Using this approach, you can be successful and achieve high conversion even with the common Google Ads campaign types.

A major brand in the finance sector achieved strong conversion with the ads targeting middle-aged people living in metropolises having high-income level.

They had to work with a different media agency regarding a special project. This agency did not bother much for this short-term campaign and targeted anyone over the age of 18.

As a result, these ads produced 7 times worse conversion compared to the brand's previous campaign.

Another brand targeting middle-aged women as the main audience got a proposal telling them how beneficial it would be to publish ads on a website and an application used extensively by 15-18 years old teenagers.

---

[22] https://www.emarketer.com/content/b23d8933-4f9b-4850-a9cd-71d3005c6f23
[23] https://www.emarketer.com/content/podcast-why-everyone-wants-personalization-but-nobody-s-getting-it

Most of the time sales professionals do not care much about formulating the right strategy, identifying the target segments and performing tests to increase conversion. They focus on selling their services.

You should prioritize the conversion perspective and arrange your campaigns accordingly.

An article on Think with Google website provided a case study.

Red Roof Inn targeted the stranded passengers at the airports because of flight cancellations. Providing a tailored message to these people such as "Stranded at the airport? Come stay with us!" enabled them to achieve a remarkable 60% increase in their bookings.[24]

You can also achieve such success.

Communicating tailored messages with segmented audiences will help you to increase your conversion rate significantly.

---

[24] https://www.thinkwithgoogle.com/marketing-resources/micro-moments/win-every-micromoment-with-better-mobile-strategy/

GOOGLE ADS PROJECT

Google Search Ads vs. SEO

The format of the search results page is changing, especially regarding certain queries.

Google focuses on the search intent of the users and displays Answer Boxes, Featured Snippets, People Also Ask, Knowledge Panel, Maps Results, and YouTube videos on the search results page, trying to provide the most accurate results in the fastest way.

While the searchers benefit from this new format, websites lose organic traffic. When Google collects, curates, and displays the information directly, there is little room left for organic rankings.

This structure brings a new challenge, even for the websites that have excellent SEO score and have the first rank on the search results page.

Even if the website is displayed at the top of the organic search results, people may still need to scroll the page to see that result.

While SEO is getting harder, Google search ads increase their importance as they are still displayed on top of the search results page.

Just look at the visual on the next page, regarding the "London hotel price" search result page on a mobile device.

london hotel price

All   Maps   News   Shopping   Images   More   Settings   Tools

About 239,000,000 results (0.57 seconds)

Cheap Hotels in London | Top Deals of the Month | trivago.com
Ad www.trivago.com/Hotels/London
trivago™ Find Your Ideal Hotel in London. Compare Prices and Save on your Stay! Free and Easy to Use. Over 1 Million Hotels. No Ads or Pop-ups. Save Time and Money. Amenities: Wi-Fi, Pool, Breakfast.
Central Hotels · Last Minute Hotels · Hotels at Great Prices · 3* Hotels · 4* Hotels · Top Rated Hotels
Cheap Hotels - from $80.00/night - Compare Prices - More

Hilton Hotels in London | Sale Now On: Save Up to 25% | hilton.com
Ad www.hilton.com/Sale/London
Book on the Official Website for Best Price Guarantee and Free Wi-Fi, Great Locations, No Booking Fees. Free WiFi. Instant Confirmation. Earn Hilton Honors Points. Outstanding Service. Best Rate Guaranteed. Amenities: Fitness Room, Meeting Rooms, Business Centre, Bar.
London Metropole Hotel · DoubleTree Kensington · DoubleTree Islington · Hilton London · Park Lane

Up To 70% Off London Hotels | Never Pay Full Price Again | goSeek.com
Ad www.goseek.com
★★★★ Rating for goseek.com: 3.9 - 202 reviews
Fresh deals. Deep discounts. Rates from £39 on London hotels with goSeek! Compare Across 200+ Sites. Over 250,000 Hotels. Hotels from £19. Exclusive Discounts. Destinations: London, Birmingham.

London Hotel Prices | Up to Half-Price on Hotels
Ad www.hotels.com/London/Hotel
★★★★ Rating for hotels.com: 4.5 - 150,401 reviews
London Hotel Prices Price Guarantee. No Reservation Costs. Budget Hotels. Earn Free Hotel Nights.

THE 10 BEST Hotels in London for 2018 (from $38) - TripAdvisor
https://www.tripadvisor.com/Hotels-g186338-London_England-Hotels.html
The #1 Best Value of 2,793 places to stay in London. Pool. Restaurant. Hotel website. Park Plaza Westminster Bridge London. Show Prices. #2 Best Value of ...
London House Hotel · Corinthia Hotel London · London marriott hotel ... Hotel 41

The 10 Best Hotels in London for 2018 | Expedia
https://www.expedia.com/London-Hotels.d178279.Travel-Guide-Hotels
View over 7867 London hotel deals and read real guest reviews to help find the ... which need upgrade at all cost as one cannot accomplish the necessary task.
1 Star Hotel in London · Apartments London · London City · London Bridge

15 Best Hotels in London. Hotels from $22/night - KAYAK
https://www.kayak.com › Hotels › United Kingdom › England
How much is a cheap hotel in London? KAYAK users have found double rooms in London for as cheap as $6 in the last 3 days. The average price is $262.

30 Best London Hotels, United Kingdom (From $29) - Booking.com
https://www.booking.com › UK › Greater London › Visit London
Great savings on hotels in London, United Kingdom online. Good availability and great rates. Read hotel reviews and choose the best hotel deal for your stay.

People also ask

What hotel to stay at in London?   ˅
What is the best hotel in London?   ˅
What are the best hotels to stay in London?   ˅
Do they have uber in London?   ˅

In this format, the users see Google Ads on top the screen, and this is all they see if they do not scroll the page.

Four Google Ads using ad extensions cover a significant area at the top.

If they scroll the page, they see the prices of hotels on Google Maps.

They see the names, visuals, prices and evaluations of some hotels selected and featured by Google. Most of the users may click on this and look closer.

If they continue scrolling, they reach the organic results.

This clearly shows how hard it is for a website that has carried out a successful SEO project and has the first spot on SERP, to get organic clicks.

Using Google Ads becomes almost inevitable in this structure.

In addition to Google search ads, you may also use local search ads which are displayed on Google Maps search pages.

As the searchers are aware that the websites using ads on the search results page are selling something, the click through rate of the ads are usually lower than the organic results.

However, ads are looking less like ads, and more like organic search results day by day.

Once, Google was displaying ads using a different background color. Today, it only uses an Ad icon looking like a piece of text on white background.

As the users have to scroll two or three times to reach organic results for certain search queries, SEO alone will not be adequate for success and digital marketing campaigns should include Google Ads to achieve the best performance.

What to Expect from Google Ads Campaigns?

The first thing you should expect from Google Ads campaigns is to achieve sustainable revenue.

This means that, depending on your perspective, short-term profit or long-term customer value should be greater than the amount of budget you spend on Google Ads.

Google Ads campaigns should provide constant revenue, without using additional budget.

Impressions, clicks (number of visitors), and bounce rate are important. You should reach your target audience, bring these people to your website, and motivate them to create engagement on your site.

The critical success factor is the conversion.

Your ads may be displayed to millions of people and you may have thousands of visitors, but this will make little sense if they do not generate any conversion.

You need to achieve sales revenue (or some kind of commercial value) to make the mechanism sustainable.

Conversions may be in the form of sales, reservations, appointments, lead forms, or phone calls.

To achieve high conversion, you should identify your target audiences correctly, provide tailored messages to each segment, and bring them to special landing pages on your website.

What Is the Value of Google Ads Campaigns?

Many brands focus on impressions and clicks in their Google Ads campaigns, but these figures are very superficial.

You may evaluate the performance of your campaigns by focusing on the complete flow.

Ads Budget	: USD 1,000
Number of clicks (visitors)	: 3,000
(Sales) Conversion Ratio	: 1%
Number of transactions	: 30
Average Order Value	: USD 150
Sales	: USD 4,500
Net profit margin	: 22,2%
Net profit	: USD 1,000

In this example, you spent 1,000 dollars, and you earned a net profit of 1,000 dollars. So, basically you earned customers without spending an additional budget.

In addition to this, you will be enjoying the lifetime value of these new customers.

Conversion ratio is the most important element in this flow.

Cost per click and average order value might be roughly similar. Conversion rate makes the difference and determines the success of the whole system. That is the reason why I am emphasizing it so much.

As long as you reach the right people and communicate the right message, at the right time, you will enjoy high conversion.

As this affects your net profit directly, it will also influence your decision about the campaign budget.

Usually, the conversion rate of ads campaigns is lower compared to direct or organic traffic.

That is mostly because the new visitors are not as eager as your regular visitors.

Also, many first-time visitors usually prefer to make a small purchase at first to test the system and to see if they will be happy with their experience regarding this ecommerce store.

Your flow may look more like this one:

Ads Budget	: USD 1,000
Number of clicks (visitors)	: 3,000
(Sales) Conversion Ratio	: 0.8%
Number of transactions	: 24
Average Order Value	: USD 120
Sales	: USD 2,880
Net profit margin	: 22,2%
Net profit	: USD 640

Obviously, this is the case if these visitors buy on their first visit.

Once they learn about your website, they may revisit your site some other time and buy at that time.

You may not see that result in Google Ads section.

If they use Google search to reach your site, you will see the last click conversion in organic traffic section. If they type your URL in the address bar, the conversion will be in direct traffic section.

In both cases, Google Ads channel will be counted as an assisted conversion, so you should also monitor that metric.

You may use remarketing ads to continue trying to convince the first-time visitors.

Once the new visitors become customers, you may enjoy lifetime value of those people.

To calculate the customer lifetime value, you can multiply average purchase value by average purchase frequency and average customer lifespan.

This provides a much larger value and you may tolerate initial low sales figures, in expectation of this higher future value.

When you calculate the customer lifetime value, you should compare it to your customer acquisition cost.

For the system to be feasible in the long run, customer lifetime value should be higher than the customer acquisition cost.

As customer lifetime value indicates a long period of time, in the short run you might be spending money and your cash flow might be negative.

If you have enough budget to support your Google ads campaigns in the short run, you may target customer lifetime value.

If your budget is limited, you may focus on short term profit.

The decision about this might vary depending on the nature of different industries.

Regarding certain businesses where the average customer lifespan is relatively long, such as car maintenance, hair salons, or local shops, you may spend more to acquire a new customer.

For a local coffee shop, if an average customer buys 50 coffees per year, with an average price of 3 dollars per coffee, for a period of 2 years, you can estimate that an average customer brings in 300 dollars revenue. If you have 20% net profit margin, you may expect to earn a net profit of 60 dollars over two years.

Regarding retail and ecommerce, you should consider your product price and profit margin to decide.

For certain categories such as food or baby products the frequency will be higher, whereas for certain products such as television or air conditioner, the frequency will be much lower.

In this case, you may focus on only the profit of that certain sales and adjust your budget accordingly.

For example, if you earn a net profit of 50 dollars from the sale of a television, that may be your limit in your ads campaign to acquire a new customer.

In addition to focusing on acquiring new customers, it is also a good idea to focus on customer retention.

Loyal customers are much likely to repurchase, or to try a new offering. They may also neglect a certain amount of price premium just to keep on shopping from a store they are used to.

You may create custom audiences using your customer database or your website visitors, and provide them additional benefits.

You may create separate campaigns for these people or increase your bids in existing campaigns for these segments.

This will help you to achieve higher conversion.

How Can You Monitor the Results?

There are two main platforms to monitor the results of your Google Ads project.

Google Analytics

This is an easy and efficient way to track performance.

If you link your Google Ads and Google Analytics accounts, you can easily track the performance of your ad campaigns on your Analytics dashboard.

You can monitor the performance of your campaigns by selecting Acquisition > Google Ads in the Analytics menu.

Analytics system also provides a secondary menu which you can monitor the performance of keywords, search queries, hour of the day, display, video or shopping campaigns.

The advantage of Analytics platform over Google Ads is that Analytics provides additional value by reporting the performance of the visitors on your website.

Here, you can see the basic site metrics such as number of users / sessions, bounce rate, pages / session, or average session duration.

Ecommerce stores can also see the ecommerce performance of ads campaigns. You can directly see the sales performance and compare this to the cost of your campaigns.

If your website is not an ecommerce store, you can still monitor the conversion rates of your goals.

Using these metrics, you can clearly see the performance of keywords and search queries. You can see which hours of the day produce good conversion. You can monitor the performance of mobile devices, computers, and tablets separately.

This is valuable information.

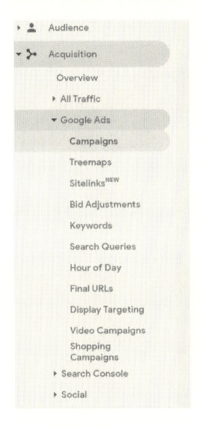

In the following chapters I will talk about campaign types and strategies.

With this tracking capability in Analytics, you can decide on the success of campaigns and perform tests to achieve the best conversion.

By selecting Acquisition > All Traffic > Source / Medium, you can compare the performance of Google Ads campaigns to other channels.

Google Ads

In addition to Google Analytics, you can monitor the performance of your campaigns directly on Google Ads.

After selecting Tools > Conversions from the menu, you may start tracking conversions.

As the first step, Google Ads system will ask you to select the kind of conversions you want to track.

You may track conversions on your website or app, track calls, or import data from another source.

In most Google Ads campaigns, the target is to achieve conversion on the website, so let's continue with that option.

The first thing is to select a conversion category. You may select the relevant category among the following options.

Sales categories: Purchase, Add to Cart, Begin Checkout, Subscribe

Leads categories: Contact, Submit Lead Form, Book Appointment, Sign-up, Request Quote, Get Directions, Outbound Click

More Categories: Page View, Other

Ecommerce stores may focus on sales categories, websites having affiliate purpose may focus on outbound clicks, real estate companies may focus on lead forms.

You should enter a name for the conversion, determine a value to measure the impact, and select count.

After creating your conversion action, Google Ads system will provide a global site tag and an event snippet.

The global site tag adds visitors to your basic remarketing lists and sets new cookies on your domain. You must install this tag on every page of your website.

The event snippet works with the global site tag to track actions that should be counted as conversions.

You need to add these codes in the <head> section of your website codes.

Which KPI's Should You Follow?

KPI is the abbreviation for Key Performance Indicator.

KPI's represent the metrics to measure performance. Using these metrics, you can compare your performance to previous periods, or you can monitor how your performance advances.

You may focus on the following KPI's in your Google Ads project:

Impressions

Every time Google Ads system displays your ad, it is called an impression.

As advertisers are eager to display their ads to their target audience, impression is a metric they monitor.

Impression is not generally as important as click through rate or conversion metric, but the ad's performance flow starts with the impression. It is the starting point.

If your aim is to reach as many people as possible and display your message or video to large audiences, it is a good idea to monitor this metric more closely.

Clicks / Click Through Rate

After an impression occurs and a user sees your ad, you should monitor if that user clicks on your ad or not.

As click through rate symbolizes the interest of the user seeing the ad, higher click through rates are better.

As this metric directly affects the quality score of your ads, it helps your ads to perform better.

Segmenting your target audience and communicating with each segment using tailored messages will help you to increase the click through rate.

As they generate revenue from the clicks, sometimes the websites in the Google display network use special tactics to make the visitors click on the ads, even if they do not want to.

In this kind of a situation, you may observe high click through rates, but you may also observe that this traffic is useless. You should be careful about this. I will elaborate on this in display ads chapter.

Impressions and click through rate will result in clicks (visitors). Together, they will provide a more detailed picture than merely the number of Google Ads visitors.

Conversions / Conversion rate

This is usually the most important metric to measure the effectiveness of the whole project.

What results do you get in the end? How profitable are Google Ads visitors?

When users click on your ad, they come to a page on your website. There, they should perform a conversion.

Conversions are the clicks resulting in a transaction and they may be in the form of sales, reservations, appointments, lead forms, or phone calls.

By placing Google Ads conversion code in your website codes, you can monitor your performance directly on Google Ads dashboard.

You should link your Google Ads and Google Analytics accounts to monitor your performance on Analytics dashboard.

You can monitor the website performance metrics of the users who click on your ads, ecommerce performance of these people, or other conversion metrics.

As the design and the functionality of your landing pages significantly affect the conversion rate, you should also focus on your website usability and website performance in general.

When you divide your cost to conversions, you have cost per conversion metric.

How much money are you spending to get one conversion? What is the value of this conversion?

The answers to these questions are important to decide on the fate of your campaigns.

User Performance: Bounce Rate, Pages/Session, Average Session Duration

Although they are usually not as important as conversions, you may monitor user performance metrics to have a better idea about the performance of your campaigns.

If the users click on your ads, come to your website, do not like what they see, you will observe high bounce rates.

As this signals an inefficient structure, it is important to monitor the campaigns having high bounce rates and work on them to improve this metric.

Pages per session indicates how many pages users visit during a session. Session duration measures the length of a visit.

You may monitor these figures on Analytics dashboard.

SCOPE OF GOOGLE ADS PROJECT

Which Products / Categories Should You Target?

Google Ads campaigns might not be applicable to all kinds of products.

In the example below, you are earning net profit because the average order value is 150 dollars and net profit margin is 22,2%.

Ads Budget	: USD 1,000
Number of clicks (visitors)	: 3,000
(Sales) Conversion Ratio	: 1%
Number of transactions	: 30
Average Order Value	: USD 150
Sales	: USD 4,500
Net profit margin	: 22,2%
Net profit	: USD 1,000

If the product price is 100 dollars and net profit margin is 10%, your net profit will be only 300 dollars and it will be far from covering the campaign budget.

If you are selling an eBook for 3 dollars (and you are not using it to sell something that has higher value), using Google ads campaigns to promote this product will be a challenge.

Ads Budget	: USD 1,000
Number of clicks (visitors)	: 3,000 people
(Sales) Conversion Ratio	: 10%
Number of transactions	: 300
Average Order Value	: USD 3
Sales	: USD 900
Net profit margin	: 50%
Net profit	: USD 450

Even if your (sales) conversion ratio is 10%, you will have 300 transactions and 900 dollars revenue. With 50% net profit margin, you will be earning 450 dollars.

You may consider brand awareness as value, but in financial terms this campaign will not be sustainable.

In summary, the products or services you advertise should generate sufficient profit to make the Google Ads campaign feasible.

Conversion rate, average order value, and net profit margin determine this net profit.

Targeting Products and Services

In the first chapter I explained that you should communicate with segmented audiences using tailored messages to achieve high conversion in your Google Ads campaigns.

To achieve this, you should first focus on the products and product categories (or services and service categories).

You should separate each product or service having a different target audience. This way, you can focus on each product or service with a different perspective.

Let's say you are managing a digital marketing campaign for a hospital. In this campaign, you need to treat every department as a separate service.

People who want to get service from different departments such as,

- Cardiology
- Diet & Nutrition
- Psychology
- Dental Health
- Urology
- Gynecology

are quite different. If you want to influence these people, you need to separate each department first.

You will then focus on targeting segmented audiences.

You will create segments and communicate with each segment using tailored messages.

For example, when working for diet & nutrition department, you will segment the audience such as:

- Women who want to lose weight
- People over 40 who are interested in healthy lifestyle and anti-aging
- Young men who focus on sports nutrition

Notice that these people are significantly different from one another and you need to differentiate your marketing message accordingly.

You can get the attention of these people by communicating the most relevant message matching their perspective.

Similarly, if you are managing a campaign for an ecommerce store selling different products, each product group addressing a different target audience should be treated separately.

Moreover, even in an ecommerce store selling only organic cosmetic products, baby products category should be separated.

Directing your audience to home page using a single marketing message never yields better results than directly showing them exactly what they are looking for.

You cannot achieve the best conversion in digital marketing campaigns by targeting wide range of audiences having different expectations and communicating a single undifferentiated message with all of these people.

Think about your products, services, and target audience.

- Do all of these people have the same characteristics?
- Will they be motivated by the same marketing message?

To be able to use tailored messages, you should separate each product or service having a different target audience.

You can perform this breakdown in various sectors.

Instead of placing different types of dresses in a single category in a fashion ecommerce store, you should use different categories for different segments such as:

- Party dresses
- Prom dresses
- Casual dresses
- Career style

Let's look from the perspective of a visitor.

A woman who searches for a party dress on Google knows exactly what she wants, and she expects to see it on the webpage she visits. You should get the attention of that person in seconds. If you display this person different types of dresses on your page, you will probably be losing a potential customer.

Even though this is the case, many websites display different types of products on a single page (probably sorted by upload date), which leads to low conversion.

You can achieve success by acting differently.

The rooms in a hotel are the same product, but -for example- the honeymoon suite is a different product targeting a specific audience.

Even though the menu is the same in a cafe, theme-based events such as the 80's night are separate services targeting different audiences.

Every fitness training program targeting a different audience is a separate product. For example, you can get the attention of older men with a special program like "Fitness Program for Men over 40". It will be much harder to influence them using a standard marketing message designed for young people in their 20s.

If you are selling computers, you should separate servers and gaming computers as different product groups.

Regarding FMCG brands, products such as whole milk, low-fat milk, and lactose-free milk are all different products targeting different segments. You can get the attention of the people in each segment using tailored messages matching their perspective.

A medical clinic organized a niche topic such as the health check for driving license as a new service. Targeting the right people, they get the attention of the people living even in distant locations. Because other healthcare institutions and hospitals were communicating undifferentiated messages with large audiences, this clinic enjoyed low competition and high conversion.

You can benefit from this approach even for business-to-business (B2B) brands using an industry-based segmentation.

A software company was successfully selling a product to the fabric companies but was having difficulty in selling that product to apparel companies.

Although the software had full compatibility for the apparel companies, they were saying "This product is not for us, it is for fabric companies.".

When the company made a few minor changes to the software and launched it as a new product targeting only apparel companies, it enjoyed high sales volume.

People demand products and services that exactly match their perspective and they are overwhelmed by the high number of messages they receive every day.

Generic marketing messages presented to large audiences are not effective anymore. You can get the attention of these people by using tailored messages.

The more accurately you segment your audience, the easier it will be to generate conversion.

SEGMENT YOUR AUDIENCE

After deciding on the products and services, you can segment your audience regarding these products and services.

As I explained in the first chapter, consumers see hundreds of messages every, they are distracted, and you should get their attention in a short period of time.

You cannot achieve this by communicating a single message with everyone.

You should segment your target audience and communicate with each segment using tailored messages to achieve the best conversion.

The benefit of segmenting your target audience is the ability to differentiate your marketing message. This will enable you to match the perspective of each target segment perfectly.

This is the only way to get the attention of people who encounter with hundreds of messages every day.

You will distinguish the right people from others, motivate them by communicating the right message and achieve conversion on your landing page.

The primary purpose of digital marketing campaigns should be to bring the "right" people to websites rather than "more" people.

If you do not segment your audience and target the right people, no matter how much traffic you create, your conversion will be low. Wrong people will not create conversion.

Therefore, the key factor for success is to identify your target segments correctly.

To do this, you need to focus on demographic, psychographic, geographic and behavioral segmentation.

You should concentrate on your existing customer profile as well as your potential customer audience.

These people may belong to the same group or they may exhibit different characteristics. For example, your existing customers might be middle-aged women, and you may want to reach younger people.

For another brand, existing customers might be tech-savvy young men and you may want to reach out to older IT professionals living in metropolises.

You may target your audience by performing the following segmentation.

Each segment should be consisting of people who will perceive your marketing message in the same way.

Each segment should be large enough to create a commercial value, should be accessible and targetable in the digital environment.

1. Demographic Segmentation: Who Is Your Target Audience?

You may begin to segment your audience based on demographic characteristics. You can do this by identifying these people.

How old are these people, what are their genders, what are their professions, what are their education level and income status, what kind of families do they have?

For example, if you are managing a digital marketing campaign for a cosmetics brand targeting young people, you may identify your segment as 18-24 years old, women, studying at universities. You may then differentiate your message based on psychographic characteristics or geographical targeting. You may also target different demographic segments such as 25-35 women, single, living in big cities, university graduate.

For a hospital, you need to target different demographic segments for each department (for example, 50+ years old men for prostate, 40+ years old office workers for back pain, 23-40 years old married women for gynecology, etc.).

For a toy company, you may present different suggestions based on the age and gender of the children. You may highlight different products based on education level and income status of the mothers.

For a white goods brand, you may formulate various segmentations such as married - single - engaged, men - women, young people - people over a certain age, people with low - high income, etc. You may highlight specific products for each segment. As these products will match their perspective perfectly, you will enjoy high conversion.

For a frozen food brand, you may target single, 25-40 years old, university graduate women, living in big cities. For the child subsegment, you may target mothers in the same regions. You may target single male segment separately.

A jewelry ecommerce store was targeting a large audience and using a single marketing message. When they targeted 18-24 years old segment for relatively cheap, colorful, trendy products, targeted 40+, university graduate, high income segment living in big cities for prestigious products, they increased their conversion significantly.

2. Psychographic Segmentation: What Kind of Personality Does Your Target Audience Have?

It is important to perform psychographic segmentation in order to thoroughly refine the segments you have identified with demographic characteristics.

What kind of personality do these people have, what are their interests, what are their lifestyles, what are their approaches to life, what are their values?

For example, if you are managing a digital marketing campaign for a home textile brand, you may differentiate your marketing message for different segments such as women having large families and traditional values, single women living in big cities preferring a modern lifestyle, young men, etc. The message you communicate with one segment will not motivate the people in other segments.

For a hospital, in addition to demographic segmentation, you may also differentiate your message based on the lifestyle of your target audience. For example, you may differentiate audiences such as smokers, fitness club members, office workers and use tailored messages that exactly match their perspective.

For an organic cosmetics brand, you may concentrate on prestigious districts in metropolises and target 25+ women who have high income, who are sensitive about protecting the nature and who are interested in a healthy lifestyle.

For a cafe or restaurant, you may communicate university students, couples, people interested in a healthy diet, fun seekers or gourmets using different messages matching their perspective.

3. Geographic Segmentation: Where Will You Reach Your Target Audience?

Once you specified the demographic and psychographic characteristics of your target audience, you need to determine the locations to reach these people.

In which countries, in which cities and in which regions in these cities do these people live?

For a luxury brand, you may target only specific prestigious districts in big cities (in addition to appropriate demographic segmentation).

For a fashion brand, you may highlight specific products in high income districts in metropolises. You may communicate different messages based on your store locations. For example, you may emphasize delivery at the store or easy return policy in cities where you have retail stores. For other cities, you may emphasize enhanced delivery features.

For a bank, you may target specific industrial areas to market SME loan products.

For a hotel, you may separately target domestic and international audiences and formulate different offers for each segment.

A university-backed dental clinic located in a central commercial district achieved significant conversion with location-based ads. They were communicating with white-collar professionals coming to work in this district in the daytime. The message was to get high-quality service in a close location from doctors who are experts in their fields. Their conversion was so high that they had to recruit extra staff.

The people you target may be at different places at different times. For example, in London, you may target different regions during business hours and during evening hours.

Similarly, you may focus on big cities in winter and vacation destinations in summer.

When you are targeting different regions, you may also differentiate your marketing message.

4. Behavioral Segmentation: What Motivates Your Target Audience to Buy?

If the people in your target audience have different motivations to buy, you need to create different segments.

This will enable you to motivate each segment using the message they want to hear.

Why do these people buy your product or service, what are the benefits they are expecting, what are their sources of motivation, at what stage of the buying process are they?

For an ecommerce store, you may categorize the people who visit the outlet page or sort the products by price as price-driven and you can formulate special offers.

You may act with the same perspective when you are targeting people who use keywords such as discount in the search query or targeting the visitors of brands selling products with lower prices.

You may separate the people who have never made a purchase and your regular customers, those who buy at the beginning of the season and those who wait for the end of season sale, VIP customers and one-time customers.

You may differentiate your site visitors and promote different messages to those who browsed a special category on your site or those who added products to their carts.

When marketing a property, you may address different expectations of those who are buying to make an investment and those who are buying to live in.

Many teenagers have strong motivation to wear the outfit of their favorite actor. For a fashion brand, you may motivate these people (those who search "coat that ...... wears" on Google, men, 18-25 years old, living in big cities) using a tailored message.

The examples in this chapter show that it is still possible to get the attention of the distracted people who encounter with hundreds of messages every day.

The key to achieve success is to identify the target segments correctly and communicate each segment using tailored messages.

This way, you will not only get the interest of these people but also motivate them to share this message with others.

A career portal published tailored ads in a selected region during the commuting time, targeting people who spent more than one hour in traffic. The message was finding a job close to home. The people were so motivated by these messages that they were showing them to other people as well.

You can create this kind of interest.

LANDING PAGES AND CONVERSION

You will reach your target audiences using Google Ads, communicate your message, and bring these people to your website to generate conversion.

You may identify the right people and use the right message at the right time, but you still have one more step. You should achieve conversion on your website.

Your website should be mobile compatible, should have high page speed, functionality, and usability.

Directing all of the Google Ads visitors to your home page will significantly decrease your conversion.

To get the attention of distracted users and to achieve the best performance, you should use landing pages.

These are special pages on your website, designed with a specific purpose, focusing on a single topic, including directions for conversion.

To achieve the best result with landing pages, you should focus on the following topics.

Create Specific Landing Pages for Each Target Segment

Remember how impatient internet users are. They are not reading thoroughly, they are glancing over content, and you should get their attention in only a few seconds.

You cannot achieve this on your home page, where there are so many messages.

Whatever message you communicate with your digital marketing campaign, you should clearly present the same message on your website. You can achieve this by bringing each target segment to a relevant landing page.

Landing pages enable you to communicate the most relevant message with each target segment.

You created specific target segments and reached them using tailored marketing messages. Now, you need to display the same messages on your website.

For a hotel, you can focus on different topics such as natural beauties, historical places, shopping, or entertainment in your Google Ads campaigns. The people having different demographic and psychographic characteristics will be motivated by different messages.

After motivating each segment using tailored messages, you may bring them to specific landing pages. You cannot achieve high conversion by bringing all of these people to your home page.

For a food brand, you can create different landing pages for people whose priorities are naturalness, freshness, health, taste or practicality. You can emphasize one aspect on each landing page, so people attaching importance to that aspect will find what they are looking for.

Everyone will be interested in the content that will match their perspective.

Think about a hotel marketing manager who visits a site presenting hundreds of articles about digital marketing. If this person sees a title like "Effective Digital Marketing Strategies for Hotels", he/she will normally be interested in that article first.

Landing pages are more effective when they are specifically designed for the target audience.

Technology brands generally use standard product pages presenting photos and specifications. However, the profile of the people who are interested in buying business computers and gaming computers are quite different.

Instead of bringing all of these people to standard pages, bringing them to a page focusing on digital games or business perspective will make a significant difference.

Ecommerce stores usually do not have special pages for the target audiences. The category and product pages have standard formats and most of the time they are limited to listing the products or providing information about the products.

Consider building permanent pages designed specifically for segments such as young men, single women, or mothers.

You may use valuable content on these pages matching the perspective of each segment. You may add blog posts and bring tailored suggestions.

You may highlight specific products for each segment and you may change these products based on your campaigns.

Doing this, you will be creating pages that each segment will visit regularly. These pages will be producing high conversion constantly.

However, many brands do not implement this.

In a study conducted globally, 78% of 5,000 consumers stated that they would shop more from retailers if those retailers offer them more focused suggestions.

However, 72% of these people also stated that online campaigns and email newsletters do not match their interests and needs.[25]

If you act differently, you can benefit from an important potential.

Be Simple. Be Direct. Be Clear.

As your Google Ads visitors are motivated by your message and visit your landing page knowingly and willingly, there is no need to use unnecessary content that is not result-oriented.

You should present the message in your ad content also on your landing page, preferably at the top. People should see it easily. This message will provide consistency. Seeing relevant content will motivate the people to stay on your website.

---

[25] https://www.infosys.com/newsroom/press-releases/Pages/digital-consumer-study.aspx

Use Powerful Headlines

When people visit your page, they will first notice headlines written in large fonts. For this reason, it is important to use a powerful and well-organized headline on each page.

You can use the message in your Google Ads campaign to provide consistency.

Focus on Visitors, Not on Yourself

Customers want to satisfy their own desires and needs. Therefore, instead of telling about yourself and the product, it will be more effective to talk about the impact of that product on the life of the person buying it.

For example, you may say "Build 1,000 business connections in just 3 days!" instead of "Our fair received awards last year.".

Increase Usability

It is important to avoid pop-ups or floating banners on the landing page unless it is absolutely necessary.

Presenting your contact information on the page and creating a structure that is easily readable on all devices will make it easier to get results.

Use Effective Visuals

Did you know that the human brain processes visuals 60,000 times faster than the text?[26] It takes only 13 milliseconds for the human brain to identify images.[27]

---

[26] https://thenextweb.com/dd/2014/05/21/importance-visual-content-deliver-effectively/
http://web.archive.org/web/20001014041642/http://www.3m.com:80/meetingnetwork/files/meetingguide_pres.pdf
[27] http://news.mit.edu/2014/in-the-blink-of-an-eye-0116

If you want to influence people in a short period of time, there cannot be a more ideal tool.

For this reason, instead of using randomly selected images on your page, you should use effective images supporting the result you want to achieve.

Act with the Conversion Perspective

What determines the fate of all your digital marketing efforts is whether the people visiting your page generate conversion or not. Therefore, this is very important.

Most of the companies give their standard content and visuals to the web agency or to the person building their website but they do not provide guidance on conversion. For this reason, in most of the cases, they end up with a website that produces very little or no conversion.

Almost all of the website owners want to promote their products and create online demand. But in most of the cases, they do not provide a clear direction to conversion, a special offer announcement, a phone number, or a short contact form on their webpages.

By doing these things, you can significantly improve your conversion.

If you want people to click on a link, you should write it in blue and make it visible. In the minds of people, the blue color is associated with the link. You can use a red button to gain attention.

If you want people to call a phone number, you should definitely use it in a mobile-friendly format. This way people can call you with a single click.

If you want people to fill out a form, you should keep this form short.

Avoid giving too many alternatives on the page, this will confuse people. Focus on a single topic. Do not distract people.

An ecommerce outlet store was bringing visitors to a page and requesting their email addresses. People could go to other pages by clicking on the top menu. When they removed the top menu from that page and simplified the conversion form to a single box, their conversion increased by 4 times.

If you do all the work and still see high bounce rates or there is little or no conversion, this could be due to two reasons: either your landing page is not well organized, or the visitors are not the right people.

In this case, you need to make revisions and try again.

SETTING CAMPAIGNS AND AD GROUPS

As Google Ads is an effective system that provides many options to segment your target audience, it is widely used on a global scale.

You can easily segment your audience and communicate each segment using tailored messages.

The first thing you should do is to create a Google Ads account and plan the campaign structure.

What Should Be the Campaign Structure?

A campaign in Google Ads is like a module. It has ad groups and ads serving for a specific purpose.

Campaigns reflect the main goal of the advertisers and the types of campaigns are based on advertising goals.

When creating a campaign, Google asks you to select the goal that would make this campaign successful to you.

Google Ads system presents the following options.

- Sales
  To drive sales online, in app, by phone, or in store

- Leads
  To get leads and other conversions

- Website traffic
  To get the right people to visit your website

- Product & brand consideration
  To encourage people to explore your products or services

- Brand Awareness & reach
  To reach a broad audience and build awareness

- App promotion
  To get more installs and interactions for your app

For ecommerce stores and retail brands you may select Sales.

For hotels, real estate companies, B2B companies, and any brand using a lead form on their website, you may select Leads.

If you are a new brand or you want more people to know about your brand, you may select brand awareness.

Technology or FMCG brands may select Website traffic or Product & brand consideration, if they do not have an ecommerce store.

As you will have multiple campaigns, you may set different goals for different campaigns.

This means that ecommerce stores may also create a campaign focusing on Brand Awareness, aiming to reach new people.

After selecting the main goal, Google Ads system displays the following options to select as the campaign type.

- Search
  To get more sales with text or call ads

- Display
  To get more sales by showing visually striking ads across the web

- Shopping
  To drive online and in-store sales

- Video
  To get more sales with video ad formats

- App
  To drive app promotion

- Smart
  To get website sales with automated ads

- Discovery
  To get more sales with visually rich personalized ads

The campaign type determines where the customers will see your ads.

For example, to achieve your Sales goal, you may be planning to reach your target audience using search, display, and shopping campaign types.

As you can adjust the settings and the budgets of the campaigns individually, you can customize each campaign based on your goals.

You should prioritize the campaigns generating high conversion and allocate your budget accordingly.

Especially if your budget is limited, it is a good idea to allocate the budget to best performing campaigns and secure that they run throughout the day.

You may create some campaigns for testing purposes, run them for some time, monitor the results, and decide based on performance.

If you are managing the campaigns for an ecommerce store selling watches in the UK, you may form campaigns based on various alternatives, such as:

Campaign 1: Search - Branded Terms
Campaign 2: Search - Watch Brands
Campaign 3: Search - Generic
Campaign 4: Shopping
Campaign 5: Display - In-market
Campaign 6: Display - Remarketing
Campaign 7: Search - Target Audience in EU
Campaign 8: Display - Target Audience in EU

I will elaborate on campaign types in detail in the following chapters.

How Should You Organize the Ad Groups?

After setting the main goal in your campaign, you can create segments by using ad groups.

Every campaign needs at least one ad group.

Ad groups enable you to target different audiences and product groups within a campaign.

For example, regarding a search campaign targeting Jackets in your ecommerce store, you may use ad groups such as;

- Leather Jackets
- Denim Jackets
- Formal Jackets

Regarding a remarketing campaign, you may target different audiences and use ad groups such as;

- All Website Visitors
- People Who Visited Shopping Cart Page
- Your Customer List

By using ad group targeting options, you can further refine your target audience and you can communicate every segment with tailored messages.

As the budget is determined at the campaign level, all of the ad groups in a campaign use a shared budget.

This may result in one ad group using all the campaign budget, leaving no room for other ad groups.

Therefore, you should monitor the performance of the ad groups closely.

An ad group contains one or more ads.

It is a good idea to use at least three ads and let the Google Ads system make a decision based on performance.

If you organize your ad groups effectively, your ads will probably have high click through rates. This will elevate your quality score and make the campaigns more efficient.

You may track the performance of each ad group on your Google Ads or Analytics dashboards.

MAIN COMPONENTS OF GOOGLE ADS CAMPAIGNS

As I explained in the previous chapter, there are various campaign types, serving different purposes.

Before focusing on each campaign type in detail, I will explain the basic settings and strategies which are applicable to all of the campaign types.

Location

When identifying your target audience in the Google Ads system, you should make segmentation based on location.

Targeting Options

Google Ads system allows you to target:

- Countries
- Areas within a country
- Radius around a location (by placing a marker on the map)

You may target the whole country or selected countries if you provide products and services to the entire country.

This option will allow you to receive more ad exposure than other options.

You may consider using more precise targeting by selecting certain regions or cities within a country.

If you are selling products or providing service in selected regions or cities, this is the obvious option.

However, you may also consider using this option to refine your target audience.

For example, you may be providing service to the entire country, but the performance of some cities may be significantly better than others. Especially if your budget is limited, you may give priority to best performing cities or regions.

Targeting the entire country will consume your budget a lot faster and will decrease your conversion rate.

If you are targeting the entire country, you may use other filters in the Google Ads system such as demographics to refine your audience.

You may use radius around a location if you are a local business that delivers within a selected radius.

This is the narrowest targeting and you will be targeting the users close to your business. You can place more than one marker on the map and select various locations.

Google evaluates various factors such as IP information and uses an estimated location for every user. At the end of the search results page, you may see that information.

Location Targeting

Google presents three options for location targeting and you can select one of them.

1. People in, or who show interest in, your targeted locations
2. People in or regularly in your targeted locations
3. People searching for your targeted locations

The first option is set as the default / recommended option and targets a wider audience. This may have advantages as well as disadvantages, depending on the nature of your business and products.

You may leave it like this for a cafe or hotel, since it may be relevant to target people searching "Oxford Street Cafe" or "hotels in London", although they are in different locations.

If you are targeting business executives in a selected district, you should change it to the second option.

A fashion brand selling men's suits targeted prestigious business districts and published ads on weekdays, from 08:00 to 18:00. They promoted slim fit suits to younger audience and higher priced products to mid-aged executives.

In their previous campaign, they were targeting everyone in that city. This approach boosted their conversion.

Hotels and real estate companies may consider using the third option to target the users who are interested in their locations.

Using location targeting, you can use the campaign budget more efficiently by eliminating the people will be less interested in your products or services.

You Can Benefit from These Strategies

The straightforward strategy is to target locations where your customers are.

If they change locations, you may target them at different locations at different times.

They can be in different districts in the city during working hours and in the evening. In winter months they can be in big cities, in summer months they can be in vacation destinations.

You can formulate a strategy by combining the location with the ad schedule. For example, for executives and mid-level managers, you can run ads targeting business districts at noon.

You can differentiate your marketing message for domestic and international customers.

You can also bring tailored suggestions to people living in cities where you have or do not have stores.

A company selling construction materials was going to open a store in a certain city. Starting from one month before opening the store they targeted the relevant audience and used Google ads heavily. Towards the opening, they announced a discount campaign just for that day and enjoyed high sales volume.

You can target the industrial zones to offer specific products or services to the factories.

You may perform even more focused targeting and select a certain location in a city, for example John F. Kennedy Airport in New York. This enables you to provide tailored solutions to the target audience.

For premium products you may target high income districts in a city, for a health clinic you may target nearby neighborhoods for basic treatments, for a cafe you may target people working in your neighborhood.

You should consider your service coverage area. If you are a local business, physical store or an ecommerce store, you should select the location accordingly.

A shopping mall was communicating with its core target audience within a 2-mile radius. Although people from other locations may also visit, they were using their energy for this audience. They were using only 10% of their budget to target people in other locations.

It is usually a good idea to include regional terms in your keyword lists when you are targeting a specific region.

For example, you may use London keyword together with car maintenance if you serve the people in London.

A dental clinic targeted its audience within a selected radius for "dental treatment" keyword. For the keyword "dental treatment + the name of the district", they were targeting the whole city.

The ad headline and ad content should be relevant to these terms to achieve the best performance.

You may also use location extensions in your ads to increase the relevance of your ads and to target locations more efficiently. I will elaborate on this in ad extensions section.

Adjusting Bids

What makes the location targeting more efficient is that you can adjust your bids for selected locations.

To optimize your campaign's budget, you can decrease bids up to 90% or increase bids up to 900%.

If you are managing a global campaign, you can easily adjust your bids based on the performance of the selected countries.

Within a country, you can perform this for selected cities or districts.

This feature will enable you to focus on best performing locations and use your campaign budget efficiently.

If you are targeting a wide area, you may choose to exclude certain locations. This will help you to focus on the people who are more likely to generate conversion.

You can see the results after you run the ads. You can perform tests regarding different locations, monitor the conversion rate and revise your ads accordingly.

Demographics

Google Ads has limited demographic segmentation options compared to Facebook, but this feature is improving day by day.

How Does Google Determine Demographic Information?

Google says that, when people are signed in from their Google Account, Google may use demographics derived from their settings or activity on Google properties.

In addition, some sites might provide Google demographic information that people share on certain websites, such as social networking sites.

Google may also use an advertising identifier linked to a customer's mobile device to remember which apps the person has used. Google then might associate the identifier with a demographic category based on web browsing and app activities on a mobile device.

For people who are not signed in from their Google Account, Google sometimes estimates their demographic information based on their activity on Google properties or the Display Network.

For example, when people browse YouTube or websites on the Display Network, Google may store an identifier in their web browser, using a "cookie."

That browser may be associated with certain demographic categories, based on sites that were visited.

As you can see, Google tracks the users heavily to understand them better.

Targeting Options

In the current dashboard, Google presents four options for demographic targeting: Age, Gender, Parental Status and Household Income.

Regarding age targeting, you may select 18-24, 25-34, 35-44, 45-54, 55-64 and 65+.

In gender section, you may target men and women.

Regarding parental status, you may select parent and not a parent. Parental status is available only for display campaigns.

Household income is a valuable targeting option. You may select top 10%, 11-20%, 21-30%, 31-40%, 41-50% and lower 50%.

You can adjust your bids for selected audiences. This enables you to focus on profitable segments and increase your conversion.

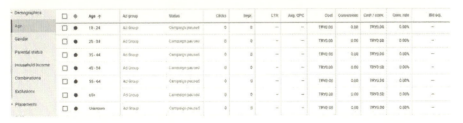

An issue with the demographic targeting is that Google does not know the demographic characteristics of a significant part of the target audience.

There is an option called "Unknown" in all of the four targeting options and usually this number is very high, especially regarding household income.

Therefore, it is a good idea to exclude only the obvious options but keep the "Unknown" option, such as only excluding men if you are selling lipstick. (There may be a small possibility of a case, such as a woman using her husband's account, but this may be negligible.).

Strategies

In the "Identifying Target Audiences" chapter, I explained the importance of identifying various segments.

Using demographic targeting options, you may perform tests and monitor the conversion of each audience.

For example, you can refine a target segment in the business districts, selecting age as 35-44, 45-54, 55-64 and 65+, and household income as top 10%, 11-20%, 21-30%. If you are selling a gender specific product or service, you may select gender. The problem here might be that these segments might be too small. Therefore, you may include the "Unknown" option.

For a fashion brand (based on the target segment of your products) you may select 18-24 years old, women. You may exclude lower 50% in household income.

For an FMCG brand, you may target 45+, women, and exclude lower 50% in household income for calcium-enriched milk product.

For a hospital, you may focus on different segments for different departments.

As an alternative to selecting only some segments, you can target all segments, but modify your bid for selected audiences.

For example, if you are selling dresses, you can select women and target all age options. You can then increase or decrease your bid for selected age groups.

If you want to communicate with these audiences using different marketing messages, you may create two campaigns.

In one campaign you may target only 18-24 age group, in other campaign you may target all other age groups by excluding 18-24 option.

After enabling the feature in Google Analytics panel in Admin > Property Settings section, you can see the age and gender distribution of your website visitors in Audience > Demographics section.

As you can clearly see the performance (website performance, goals, or ecommerce performance) of each age and gender group, you can easily adjust bids to focus on best performing audiences.

This will help you to achieve maximum conversion.

Devices, Operating Systems and Networks

Devices

Google Ads system enables you to target (or exclude) four types of devices in Devices menu.

- Computers
- Mobile Phones
- Tablets
- TV Screens

You can choose appropriate devices based on your campaign and adjust your bids for these devices accordingly.

Device	Level	Added to	Bid adj.	Ad group bid adj	↓ Clicks	Impr.	CTR	Avg. CPC	Cost	Conversions	Cost / conv.	Conv. rate
Computers	Campaign	Sample Campaign	--	None	0	0	--	--	TRY0.00	0.00	TRY0.00	0.00%
Mobile phones	Campaign	Sample Campaign	-30%	I ad group	0	0	--	--	TRY0.00	0.00	TRY0.00	0.00%
Tablets	Campaign	Sample Campaign	--	None	0	0	--	--	TRY0.00	0.00	TRY0.00	0.00%
TV screens	Campaign	Sample Campaign	--	None	0	0	--	--	TRY0.00	0.00	TRY0.00	0.00%
Total: Ca...					0	0	--	--	TRY0.00	0.00	TRY0.00	0.00%

As a general strategy, it is a good idea to start the campaign on all devices, monitor the conversion closely, and decide based on the performance.

Mobile phones usually generate lower conversion than computers. Therefore, you may lower your CPC bidding by 20% to 50% on mobile devices.

This way, mobile ads will attract more visitors with the same budget.

Although the conversion is lower than computers, the number of clicks will be higher, and the sales to cost ratio becomes more balanced.

If you do not want any mobile traffic, you may set the bidding as minus 100%.

If you want to target only mobile visitors, you may do this to other devices.

Using this option, you may create two separate campaigns, one for mobile, one for tablet & computers. You may focus on different products or marketing message.

As the share of mobile devices in total website visits often exceeds 60% for ecommerce stores, it makes sense to focus on mobile devices and customize your message accordingly.

You can monitor the performance of devices in the Audience > Mobile section of your Google Analytics panel and adjust the bids based on performance.

Device Models, Operating Systems, and Network Selection

For display ads campaigns, Google Ads system provides Devices option in Settings menu.

This option enables you to set specific targeting for devices.

You can choose the mobile operating system or even target a specific device.

In the previous section, I explained that the Google Ads system provides little information regarding household income.

By selecting only certain devices (such as iPhone 11), you can use another targeting option to target high income segment. This may be a good strategy to refine your audience.

Google Analytics reports the performance of devices in the Audience > Mobile > Devices section.

This will allow you to monitor the performance of specific devices such as Apple iPhone. If you see an opportunity regarding certain devices, you can target only those devices in your Google Ads campaign.

75

You can set the operating system as Android, BlackBerry, Windows Phone, iOS, or webOS.

If you sell an eBook on Apple Books and Google Play Books, or if you manage a campaign for a mobile app, this targeting will be extremely helpful.

For certain countries, you can also choose the network.

You should try different scenarios, closely monitor your conversions on Google Ads and Analytics dashboards and update your campaign settings based on performance.

Language

You can target your audience based on language.

On the search network, Google Ads uses a variety of signals to understand which languages the user knows, and attempts to serve the best ad available in a language the user understands.

These signals may include query language, user settings, and other language signals as derived by machine learning algorithms.

On the Google Display Network, Google Ads may detect and look at the language of pages or apps that the user is viewing or has recently viewed, to determine which ads to show.

Based on your campaign settings, Google displays your ads targeting these users.

You may use various strategies regarding language option.

If you are running global campaigns, this selection is important. If your website is in English, you should use your ads in English and only select English as the language in campaign settings.

If you are promoting an eBook written in English, you should act the same way.

You may also use language selection to target a specific audience in another country, for example French people living in Germany.

If you manage campaigns for an ecommerce store in France, you can expand your audience using this strategy.

If you are selling products specific to France, you may target a homesick audience using a theme such as "feeling at home".

This strategy will also generate high conversion when you target Arab or Indian population in the UK regarding specific ethnic products.

Using this feature, you can select a touristic location and target the people using -for example- French on their mobile devices, to target specific tourists.

Cafes, restaurants, city tours, or souvenir shops may benefit from this strategy. Instead of sitting and waiting for tourists to discover their location, they may actively communicate with the target segment.

If your business provides service in additional languages, you may promote this. For example, if a health clinic in Greece has German speaking staff, this will affect the decision of the German people positively.

If you are living in a country other than Australia, Canada, US or UK, you may benefit from language selection to refine your audience.

Even if you are targeting a local audience, by selecting English as the language, you may elevate the target segment. These people usually have higher income and higher level of education. You may exclude 18-24 age group to exclude students.

You may also use this mentality to exclude selected audiences.

For example, based on your products you may exclude Arabic, Indian languages when you are managing a campaign in UK.

Ad Schedule

Ad scheduling enables you to determine the time when you want your ads to run.

You can select specific days and hours within a week, run or pause your campaign at these times, or adjust your bids.

Ad schedules are set at the campaign level.

To use an ad schedule for a campaign, you can simply select the campaign and Ad Schedule from the main menu.

Keep in mind that ad schedule uses the time zone you selected when you create your Google Ads account.

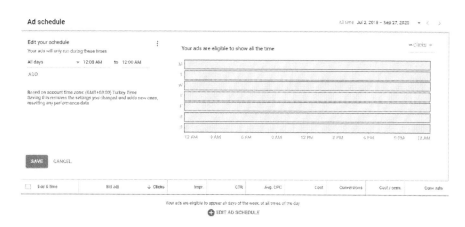

Before working on the ad schedule, you should review your sales performance on Analytics panel.

Which days and hours do your customers prefer? Is there a difference between weekend and other days, or morning, business hours and evening?

The straightforward strategy is to increase your bids targeting the time periods when you have high sales and decrease your bids for time periods when you have low sales.

For example, if your sales numbers are not that great at the weekends, you may decrease your bid by 30%. This way, you will still be presenting your ads to the target segment, but you will not be that ambitious regarding ad rankings. You may have lower impressions but a better conversion rate or cost per acquisition.

If your budget is limited and finishes in the afternoon, but if you have good conversion in the evening, it becomes more important to manage the timing to use your budget efficiently.

Depending on your sales data, you may pause your ads in selected days or hours, for example weekends or nights.

You may choose daytime hours to target businesspeople in their workplaces. For mid-level and senior managers, you may prefer noon or an hour before and after regular business hours.

A dental clinic operating in a business district was running ads only in business hours, targeting businesspeople. Using a tailored message for these people, they enjoyed high conversion.

When targeting mothers, you may pay attention to the sleep time of children and communicate your message at that time.

You should also consider your customer service hours.

For example, if you manage ads campaign for a restaurant, you should consider running ads when you open and pause them about an hour before closing.

If you use a telephone number in your ads, you should make sure that someone answers that line when your ads are running.

For special days such as the Valentine's Day, you may start 10 days before that time and stop based on your delivery capability. As this is a special day, the audience will be very sensitive to on-time delivery.

As ad schedules can limit the reach of your ads, you may choose not to use this option if there is no clear difference in your sales or conversion data.

Budget

Budget is determined at the campaign level in Google Ads.

You set the aim in your campaigns, identify the audience to reach, and determine how aggressive you will be in reaching these people. These will determine your budget.

If you plan to reach a wide audience and want to rank on top of the search results for a wide range of keywords, you will need a high budget.

Since the company executives are not familiar with the Google Ads working principles, they usually want to rank high for various generic keywords. This results in high cost per click and low conversion.

You need to focus on the performance to achieve budget efficiency.

If there are too many campaigns, the budget may not be enough. If your bids are too low, ads will not be displayed.

For this reason, it is necessary to determine the most efficient campaigns based on the performance. These campaigns should be planned so that they receive enough clicks and run throughout the day.

At the initial stage, the campaigns are set using predictions. As they run and produce results, you may revise your campaigns by monitoring the performance.

In the "What Is the Value of Ads Campaigns?" section, I provided a sample cost/profit flow.

Your net profit will be determining the ads budget in the long term and this profit is affected by your conversion rate.

Many brands say they have limited ads budgets and some of them are reluctant to advertise on Google. This is before they see the performance.

If they see that the ads campaigns generate them 5 or 10 dollars sales revenue for every 1 dollar they spent, they impose no limits on the budget.

A men's fashion brand was using big budgets for Google Ads campaigns, but the executives were not happy with the results. They were thinking of lowering the budget.

The problem was they were using a significant amount of the budget for display ads targeting a wide audience and that was not producing good results.

When they changed the structure and revised targeting options for their campaigns, they immediately achieved a 40% increase in their conversions. What happened then? They increased the budget instead of decreasing it.

Planning the right campaign and ad group structure is important to achieve the best performance.

There may be high number of ad groups in each campaign. If an ad group has wide targeting and uses all the campaign budget, ads in the other ad groups will not be displayed.

You should monitor the performance of the ad groups and if such a situation occurs, you should try to narrow your targeting or consider creating a separate campaign for that ad group.

Bidding

In the past, advertisers were using mostly manual bidding in Google Ads campaigns. As the machine learning and automatic systems evolve and begin to understand the user actions better, automatic bidding options began to dominate the Google Ads system.

Google Ads offers bid strategies that are tailored to different types of campaigns. Each bid strategy is suited for different kinds of campaigns and advertising goals.

I will present the current alternatives below and talk about the effectiveness of each alternative after this part.

Cost per Click Bidding (focus on clicks)

Manual CPC Bidding

In this option, you can manage your maximum CPC bids yourself. You can set different bids for each ad group in your campaign, or for keywords or placements.

Maximize Clicks

This is an automated strategy. You set an average daily budget, and the Google Ads system automatically manages your bids to bring you the most clicks possible within your budget.

Smart Bidding (focus on conversions)

Enhanced CPC

This option will automatically adjust your bids. The algorithm may alter the bid for clicks that seem more or less likely to lead to a conversion on your website.

It is an optional feature you can use with Manual CPC bidding.

Target CPA (cost per action)

With this bidding, Google Ads automatically sets bids to help get as many conversions as possible at the target cost-per-action (CPA) you set.

Maximize Conversions

This option works like Target CPA. The difference is that it aims to optimize for conversions for your entire budget instead of targeting a specific CPA. So, you do not set a Target CPA level, you leave the decision to Google.

Target ROAS (Return on Ad Spend)

If you want to optimize for conversion value, you can use this option. The system works to increase the conversion value while targeting a specific return on ad spend. You set this number.

Maximize Conversion Value

This option works like Target ROAS. The difference is that it aims to optimize for conversion value for your entire budget instead of targeting a specific ROAS. So, you do not set a Target ROAS level, you leave the decision to Google.

Impressions (focus on visibility)

Target Impression Share

This option automatically sets bids with the goal of showing your ad on the page of Google search results.

You have the option to select the place as absolute top of the page, top of the page, or anywhere on the page.

CPM

With this bid strategy, you will pay based on the number of impressions (times your ads are shown) that you receive on YouTube or the Google Display Network.

vCPM

Viewable CPM impressions bidding optimizes your bids so your ads show in ad slots that are more likely to become viewable.

Google evaluates an ad as viewable when 50% of it has been on screen for one second or more.

So, you don't pay when the ad impression is not viewable.

Video Views / Interactions (focus on views or interactions)

This option is applicable to video ads. With CPV bidding, you will pay for video views and other video interactions. You set the highest price you want to pay for a view.

So, Which Bidding Option Should You Use?

Google bidding options may seem confusing. There are many options resembling each other and it may be hard to decide on which one to use.

The first thing you should do is to decide on the aim of your campaign. What do you want to focus on?

Do you want to achieve conversion, create traffic, or reach as many people as possible?

Ecommerce stores, hotels, training companies, event companies, real estate companies may focus on conversion. As Google system needs some time to learn the campaign and to optimize it for conversion, these companies may start with focusing on traffic first. After some time, they may switch to conversion bidding.

FMCG, automotive, or healthcare brands may focus on traffic if they do not have the tools on their websites to generate leads.

New brands or movie producers may focus on impressions and creating awareness.

Automated bidding strategies are easy to use.

However, especially at the initial stage of your campaign, the automatic CPC rises to very high levels compared to manual CPC strategy.

For example, you may be paying 0.50 dollars per click using manual CPC. Automated bidding may increase this level to 3 or 5 dollars per click.

If your budget is limited, automated bidding can easily consume that budget in a short period of time without creating conversion. This may lead to inefficient results.

For this reason, it may be better to use manual bidding at the initial stage of your campaigns.

If you do not have a budget constraint, you may begin with Enhanced CPC strategy. After running the campaign for some time and letting Google Ads system learn about your clicks and conversion, you may switch to a more result-oriented option such as maximize conversions, maximize conversion value, or target ROAS.

If you select maximize conversions, Google Ads systems works to provide you the maximum number of conversions. This will be appropriate for businesses such as hotels or training companies which try to generate leads.

For ecommerce stores, it is a better idea to give priority to maximize conversion value or target ROAS. This time, Google Ads systems will work to provide you the highest value, increasing sales volume.

Average cost per click in Google Ads campaigns obviously changes based on industries and target keywords.

To give you an idea, some researches state the average CPC around 2-3 dollars for the search campaigns in the US. This figure may be below this level for some ecommerce products and may exceed 5 dollars in legal service ads.

On the bidding page, if you select "or, select a bid strategy directly (not recommended)" option, you can set a maximum cost per click bid limit.

Although Google Ads system does not recommend this, you may use it to keep the CPC level under control.

If you prefer manual bidding strategy, you set the maximum CPC bid manually. As the Google Ads system is very dynamic and competition always changes, you should constantly monitor your bids in your campaigns.

As a starting strategy, instead of paying very high CPC to generic keywords, it would be more appropriate to focus on the result-oriented (long tail) keywords that matches the perspective of the target audience and allocate your budget on these keywords.

The advantage of manual bidding is to focus on certain keywords and limit your maximum CPC.

On the other hand, especially if you have high number of campaigns, it will be hard to achieve high efficiency.

Audiences

Google Ads systems presents Audience Manager in Tools & Settings menu.

In this section, you can create audiences based on different data sources, and target these audiences in your Google Ads campaigns.

This will enable you to reach people based on their interests and habits, what they are actively researching, or how they have interacted with your business. You can also target users who resemble your visitors.

In this section I will talk about the general functioning mechanism of the audiences. I will talk about the most effective strategies in following chapters, when I talk about campaign types.

The most common data sources are Google Ads tag, Google Analytics, YouTube, Google Play, App analytics, and your customer data.

If the data sources do not have enough information (for example if there are too few visits), you may see "Too small to serve" message in your panel.

Remarketing (Website Visitors, App or YouTube Users)

You may target the users who are familiar with your brand or your website.

When you place Google Ads tracking code (or Google Tag Manager code) in the codes of all of your website pages, Google Ads system can track users.

You can then target all of your website visitors, users visiting specific pages, or users completing a certain conversion on your website.

As the users usually visit more than one website before buying a product or a service, you may outrank your competitors by using remarketing feature and being persistent.

By targeting the users visiting specific pages on your website, you can present tailored messages.

You can also create special audiences by targeting the users who downloaded your app or who interacted with your YouTube Channel or videos.

Customer Lists

You may upload your customer list to the Google Ads system to create a special audience. This information is usually in the form of email addresses or phone numbers.

This will allow you to continue communicating with your customers on digital platforms.

You should make sure that you have the necessary permissions to use their information.

Customer lists are powerful, and they usually produce high conversion. For this reason, they should be part of any Google Ads campaign.

Similar Audiences

Google Ads system automatically creates similar audiences based on your audiences.

This may be a good opportunity as you can target people who are not your customers or who have not come your website, but who are similar to them.

Google Ads system monitors the browsing activity of the users to understand the shared interests and characteristics of the people in your list.

Based on this information, it automatically finds new potential customers whose interests and characteristics are similar to the people in your list.

It is usually a good option because it enables you to reach out to new people and these people may act the same way as your customers.

Your existing customers may still generate better conversion, but you need to increase the number of new users to grow your platform.

To increase the efficiency of this mechanism, it is a good idea to target the similar audience of a narrow audience, such as your visitors who visited the shopping cart page.

As the number of all website visitors is high and these people show different characteristics, similar audience may not yield good results.

You may give priority to a longer-term communication plan when you are targeting new audiences. You may introduce yourself first, then talk about your advantages.

If your prices are lower compared to your competitors, similar audiences usually produce good results. If your prices are higher, you need to use additional targeting options to refine this audience.

Custom Audiences

You may create custom audiences in the Audience Manager, aiming to target the people who did not visit your website and who are not your customers.

Google Ads system presents two options to create these audiences.

1. People with any of these interests or purchase intentions

You simply enter names of your products or customer's interests as keywords and Google creates a custom audience targeting the people who show interest or purchase intention regarding these keywords.

2. People who searched for any of these terms on Google

By targeting keywords in search campaigns, your ad is displayed to the searchers when they perform the search.

When you enter your target keywords in this section, Google creates a custom audience targeting people who performed those searches before.

You need to be careful with this option. The user might already have bought the product after performing the search and might not be interested in your message.

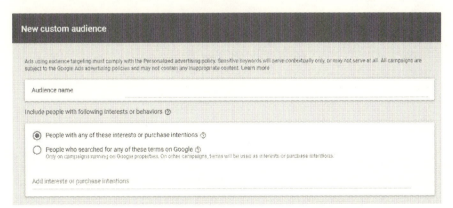

In addition to these two options Google Ads system presents some additional options to expand the audience.

People who browse types of websites option enables you to enter the website addresses (URLs) that your ideal customer might visit.

People who use types of apps option enables you to enter the names of apps that your ideal customer might use.

People who visited certain places option enables you to enter the types of places where your ideal customer might spend time.

These places may be Hostels, Travel Accommodations, Indian Restaurants, Resorts, Restaurants, Hotels, Retailers & Shops, Motels, Farmers Markets, Budget Hotels.

These additional options may help you to reach new audiences effectively.

For example, by targeting the website addresses (URLs) of your competitors, you may try to reach their visitors. This may produce good results.

If you manage the campaign for a local business, you may benefit from people who visited certain places option.

Audience Targeting

You can use Audiences menu in a campaign to select your target audiences.

As display ad campaigns generally produce weak conversion, it is important to identify and refine the audiences correctly.

For search ad campaigns you can also combine these audiences, and this will help you to increase your conversion.

Affinity Audiences

Affinity audiences enable you to reach people based on their lifestyles, passions, and habits. These users are passionate about a specific topic or area of interest.

Google Ads system presents the following main categories as affinity audiences.

Banking & Finance, Beauty & Wellness, Food & Dining, Home & Garden, Lifestyles & Hobbies, Media & Entertainment, News & Politics, Shoppers, Sports & Fitness, Technology, Travel, Vehicles & Transportation.

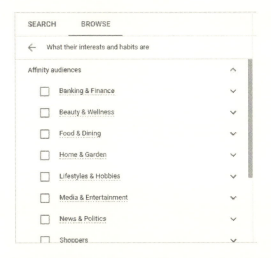

You may also select a specific subcategory instead of a main category. For example, when you click on the Shoppers category, Google Ads system presents the following subcategories.

Bargain Hunters, Luxury Shoppers, Shopaholics, Shoppers by Store Type, Convenience Store Shoppers, Department Store Shoppers, Superstore Shoppers, Value Shoppers.

As the people in subcategories such as Bargain Hunters and Luxury Shoppers have significantly different characteristics, it will be better to target the appropriate subcategory instead of the main category.

In-market Audiences

This audience type represents the users who are in the market and searching for products or services to buy.

Google Ads system evaluates various factors such as search queries and browsing history of the user and decides to include that user in the list or not.

For example, if a person is browsing shopping ads, reading reviews and watching comparison videos about certain products Google might decide to include that person in the in-market audience list.

As you can target users on their shopping journey, these audiences enable you to target the audience at the right time.

Google Ads system presents the following main categories as in-market segments.

Apparel & Accessories, Arts & Crafts Supplies, Autos & Vehicles, Baby & Children's Products, Beauty & Personal Care, Business & Industrial Products, Business Services, Computers & Peripherals, Consumer Electronics, Dating Services, Education, Employment, Event Tickets, Financial Services, Gifts & Occasions, Home & Garden, Musical Instruments & Accessories, Real Estate, Seasonal Shopping, Software, Sports & Fitness, Telecom, Travel.

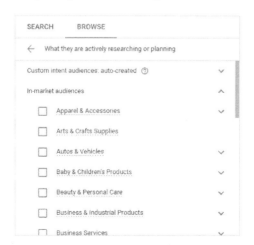

As these categories enable broad targeting, you may also select a specific subcategory instead of a main category.

For example, when you click on the Apparel & Accessories category, Google Ads system presents the following subcategories.

Activewear, Backpacks, Costumes, Eyewear, Formal Wear, Handbags, Hats, Jewelry & Watches, Lingerie, Luggage, Men's Apparel, Outerwear, Pants, Shirts & Tops, Shoes, Socks, Swimwear, Underwear, Wallets, Briefcases & Leather Goods, Women's Apparel.

As the people in subcategories such as Men's Apparel and Women's Apparel have significantly different characteristics, it will be better to target the appropriate subcategory instead of the main category.

Life Events

Google Ads system presents the following main categories as life events.

Business Creation, College Graduation, Job Change, Marriage, Moving, Purchasing a Home, Retirement.

The subcategories enable you to refine the target audience.

You can select Getting Married Soon or Recently Married, Purchasing a Home Soon or Recently Purchased a Home, Recently Retired or Retiring Soon.

Communicating with these people using tailored messages will provide high conversion.

Detailed Demographics

As I explained in the Demographics targeting section, you can select Age, Gender, Parental status and Household income in the Demographics menu.

Google Ads system also enables you to target Detailed Demographics options in the Audiences section.

You can select Parental Status, Marital Status, Education, and Homeownership Status.

Subcategories enable you to refine the audiences such as Parents of Infants (0-1 years), Parents of Toddlers (1-3 years), Parents of Preschoolers (4-5 years), Parents of Grade-Schoolers (6-12 years), Parents of Teens (13-17 years).

Keywords

In search ad campaigns, keywords add another layer of targeting to audiences.

Google Ads system does not display your ads to everyone searching for those keywords.

If the users performing the searches for those keywords are also in your target audience, then Google displays the ad.

Observation vs. Targeting Options

You have two options when you are targeting the audiences: Targeting and Observation.

You may target multiple audiences, selecting from affinity audiences, detailed demographics, in-market audiences, remarketing and similar audiences.

If you select the "Targeting" option, Google Ads system will target the people who match any of the selected audiences. It does not narrow down the audience to the people who are included in all of these groups.

For example, if you target Shoppers (affinity audience) + Toys (in-market audience > baby category > toys), Google Ads system targets all the shoppers + all the people in the market looking for toys.

For this reason, it is a better idea to limit your targeting, for example by selecting only in-market audiences. You may target one audience to clearly observe its performance.

If you select various audiences, you may try to refine this group by using other targeting options, such as demographics, locations, or devices.

If you want to target people satisfying all of the selected options, you should use combined audiences. I will elaborate on that topic in the following section.

If you select the "Observation" option, Google Ads system will not narrow the reach of your ad group based on your selection.

It will only report the performance of selected audiences separately for observation purpose.

You may use this option to observe the performance of different target segments.

If some of these segments generate good conversion, you may use "Targeting" option for those audiences in separate campaigns.

Google Ads system enables you to adjust your bids based on selected audiences.

You may monitor the performance and increase your bids for the best performing audiences

How Can You Combine Audiences?

As I explained in the previous section, "Observation" option does not affect the audience targeting.

By selecting "Targeting" option, you may target various segments. This time, you will be targeting all of those segments.

What if you want to target audiences that satisfy all of those targeting options? You use combined audiences.

Google presents this option for search campaigns.

After selecting Audiences from the menu, you will see "Search and Browse" just below "Targeting and Observation" options. You should select Browse > Combined Audiences > New Audience.

After selecting an audience, you should click on "Narrow Your Audience (And)" link and add another audience.

Google Ads system will target the people who are in all of these segments.

Using combined audiences will help you to improve the performance of your campaigns. You may create well targeted audiences and use tailored messages to get the attention of these people.

For example, let's say you are selling toys.

You create a search campaign, use "toy" keyword and target all of the searchers who use this keyword in search query.

With this targeting, you will be spending thousands of dollars and probably will not be achieving a meaningful sales revenue.

Now, let's think that you use combined audiences.

You can target Parents of Infants (0-1 years) + Luxury Shoppers + In-market audience who are actively searching to buy Toys.

You will enjoy high conversion when you use a tailored message and bring these people to a relevant page on your website.

Targeting combined audiences provides enormous power to marketers.

You should benefit from this targeting to increase the conversion in your search campaigns.

I will talk about the strategies in Search Ads chapter.

GOOGLE SEARCH ADS

Every day more than 6 billion searches are performed on Google.

This excites the website owners. They want to be on top of the Google search results and attract visitors to their websites.

This creates significant competition.

The number of indexed pages on Google was only 26 million in 1998. This number exceeded 1 trillion in 2008 and reached 130 trillion in 2016.[28]

Everyone thinks that their products and services are great, and Google should immediately rank their websites on top of search results, but this is very hard to achieve.

Search ads is a fast and easy alternative to organic rankings. Obviously, you will be using a budget for this.

In the "Google Search Ads vs. SEO" section I explained that the format of the search results page is changing, especially regarding certain queries. As Google displays Answer Boxes, Featured Snippets, People Also Ask, Knowledge Panel, Maps Results, and YouTube videos on the search results page, it is hard for organic results to get clicks.

---

[28] https://searchengineland.com/googles-search-indexes-hits-130-trillion-pages-documents-263378

Therefore, you should consider using search ads, especially for result oriented target keywords.

To achieve the best conversion and maximize your success, you should pay attention to the following topics.

Networks

Google Search Results Page, Search Network, Display Network

Based on the name, many people think that Google Search Ads are displayed only on Google search results page.

However, the reach is significantly wider as Google also uses Search Network and Display Network to display search ads.

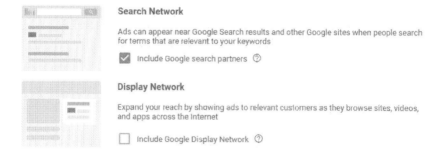

Google Search Network are the websites that partner with Google to show ads on their search results.

Google displays your ads on these websites when people search for terms that are relevant to your keywords.

Google Display Network is a collection of more than 2 million websites, videos, and apps.

By using this network, Google expands your reach by showing ads to relevant customers as they browse sites, videos, and apps across the web.

How Can You Monitor the Data?

If you select search partners in your search ads campaign, you can see the performance in Google Ads dashboard.

When you selected the campaign, you may simply click on Segment icon and select Network (with search partners) option.

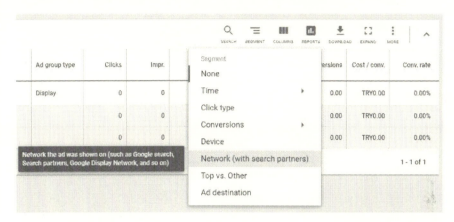

Google Ads system will provide a performance breakdown of ads. Here you can monitor cost, conversion, conversion rate, and cost/conversion metrics.

Performance and Conversion

Search Network and Display Network usually provide lower conversion compared to Google search results page.

The performance of Display Network is usually worse than Search Network (as the target users are not actively performing a search).

Google might think it is relevant and display your ads on selected Display Network websites, but these sites may have a different audience, or users might be browsing those websites with a different purpose. They might not be interested in your messages.

The ads in the Search Network and Display Network might have lower click through rate, fewer clicks, and lower conversion rate.

However, as they also have lower cost per click compared to Google search, cost/conversion metric might be balanced.

Therefore, it is important to test these options and observe the performance. You should focus on cost/conversion metric to make the right decision.

Decision and Strategies

Google Ads system automatically selects all available options when you are creating a search ad campaign to provide the largest reach.

Google's priority may be providing the largest reach, but your priority is to achieve high conversion. As I explained in the previous section, your priority should be cost/conversion metric.

As the search queries including your brand name represent the people who are familiar with your brand, it is a good idea to use the Search Network for these searches without restricting your target audience. For keywords other than branded terms this may lower your conversion.

If you are managing the campaigns for a result-oriented business such as an ecommerce store and if using your budget efficiently is important, you should give priority to this.

You may start the campaign by using only Google search for some time. After monitoring the cost/conversion metric, you may test the efficiency of Search Network and Display Network.

If they consume your budget fast and does not generate meaningful conversion, you may turn these options off.

When you are using these options, it is good idea to refine the audience by selecting other relevant Google Ads targeting options. For example, you may select high income group using specific devices, living in high income districts.

This will help you to achieve higher conversion.

KEYWORD STRATEGIES

As the search ads are based on keywords, selecting the right keywords and formulating effective strategies are important to maximize the performance of campaigns.

You should focus on following topics to achieve the best performance.

Keyword Matching Options

The Google Ads system recognizes keywords in four different matching options.

You can control the searches triggering your ad by using keyword match types.

Broad Match: For example, women's dress

If you use broad match format, your ad is eligible to serve when someone searches for relevant variations of your keyword.

This system where you leave the control to Google Ads, provides the widest targeting.

This option helps you to target more users, spend less time building keyword lists.

It is simple and easy to use, but generally it provides the lowest conversion among keyword matching options.

As Google Ads system decides on the relevance of the search query, it tends to display your ad without restricting the audience too much.

You may waste your money on irrelevant keywords and your conversion may be low because of this.

In this format you only write the keywords, without using any marks, such as women's dress.

When you target this keyword, your ad may also be displayed to the people using different search queries such as:

- fashion events
- women's clothing stores in London
- photos of evening dresses
- dress blogs
- maxi dresses
- mini dresses
- plus size dress
- various brand names
- women's dress games

Needless to say, most of these searchers will not create conversion as they are searching for something else.

Unless you have a specific purpose, it is a good idea to avoid broad match format in your campaigns.

This may seem less important for branded terms. Normally branded terms are highly efficient and produce significant conversion.

However, when Google Ads matches your brand name with keywords such as plus size fashion or plus size dresses, this will significantly increase the cost per click and decrease the conversion in your branded campaigns.

For other campaigns, this is more important. For example, if you are selling jeans, you do not want your ads to be displayed to people searching for other types of trousers.

In certain situations, to observe which keywords your target users are using, to understand their perspective, to discover the keyword alternatives, you may use broad match format with a limited budget for testing purposes.

In a sense, you will be spending money on R&D.

Broad Match Modifier: For example, +women's +dress

Broad match modifiers ensure your ads to be displayed for searches that include the words you mark with a plus sign.

In other words, every word after the plus sign must be included in the search query in order for your ad to be displayed.

Broad match modifiers help you to communicate with a more targeted audience and may increase the click through rate of your ads.

In this format the plus sign should be adjacent to the keywords, such as +women's +dress. You should not leave space between the + sign and the keyword.

When you target this keyword, every search query including the words "women's" and "dress" will trigger your ad.

Your ad may be displayed to the people using search queries such as:

- women's clothing style and dress models
- women's dress stores in London
- women's dress stores in Dublin
- plus size women's dress brands
- blogs about women's dress
- women's dress games

If only some of the terms in your keyword have + sign, such as +women's long +dress, then the terms without the + sign will be treated as broad match.

This means your ad may be displayed for search queries such as +women's maxi +dress.

This keyword matching option yields better results compared to broad match format, but you still may get some irrelevant clicks.

When using this option, you should constantly review the search terms. By selecting Keywords > Search Terms in Google Ads menu, you can see which terms generate traffic to your website. You can monitor the impressions and clicks.

If some of these search terms do not match with your products, you should mark them as negative keywords and remove them from your campaign.

If necessary, you may use more words with the plus sign for a better match, such as +women's +long +dress or +women's +maxi +dress .

The number of impressions will be reduced but right people will be seeing your ad.

Phrase Match: For example, "women's dress"

With phrase match, you can show your ad to users who are searching for that keyword. There may be additional words before or after this keyword.

In this format you use the keyword in quotation marks, such as "women's dress".

Regarding our example, any search combination that includes "women's dress" phrase will trigger your ad.

Your ad may be displayed to the people using search queries such as:

- women's dress celebrity style
- women's dress photos
- blogs about women's dress
- plus size women's dress
- women's dress games

Phrase match is more targeted than the broad match, but more flexible than exact match.

When you use a good negative keywords list, it will be possible to get good results.

Google says that with phrase match, your ad can appear when people search for your phrase and close variations of that phrase. Close variants include misspellings, singular and plural forms, acronyms, stemmings, abbreviations, accents, implied terms, synonyms and paraphrases, and variants of your keyword terms that have the same meaning.

Based on this, Google also says that if your target "tennis shoes" keyword as the phrase match, your ads may be displayed for searches such as "comfortable tennis sneakers".

This means that although you use phrase match, Google may still display your ad for a relevant search query.

For this reason, you should constantly review the search terms and if there are irrelevant words, you should mark them as negative keywords.

Exact Match: For example, [women's dress]

This is the narrowest match.

With exact match, you can show your ad to users who are searching for that exact keyword.

In this format, you use the keyword in brackets, such as [women's dress].

The disadvantage of this matching option is to limit yourself too much. The search volume for the keywords may be low. In this case, you will not be wasting your money, but you will not be reaching to your target audience either.

Google Ads system displays the ad for close variants of that keyword. Close variants include searches for keywords with the same meaning as the exact keyword.

Google says that when you use [shoes for men] exact match targeting, your ads may be displayed for searches such as shoes men, men shoes, men shoe, or shoes for a man.

Free Sites and Tools for Keyword Research

Google Ads Keyword Planner

This is a useful tool to see the possible results of your keywords.[29]

Keyword Planner presents two options for keyword research.

1. Discover new keywords

This is a very useful tool.

You simply enter your target keywords and this tool provides you average monthly search volume, competition level, top of the page bid for those keywords.

It also provides these results for a high number of related keywords and presents them as keyword ideas.

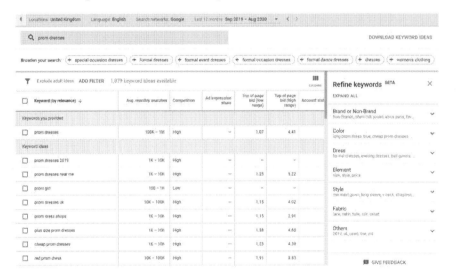

You may add new keywords to broaden your search.

You can also refine the keywords by selecting certain groups.

---

[29] https://ads.google.com/home/tools/keyword-planner/

You can clearly see the popularity and search volume of the target keywords, understand the competition, and see top of the page bid levels.

2. Get search volume and forecasts

You set the location, language and the search network, and this tool provides estimated figures for clicks, impressions, cost, click through rate, average cost per click, and average position, based on your target keywords.

Google says that forecasts are updated daily with data from the last 7-10 days.

MOZ Keyword Explorer

MOZ requires Pro membership for most of its tools.

Free members can analyze 10 search queries using Keyword Explorer as a free tool.[30]

Keyword Explorer provides monthly volume, difficulty, and organic CTR metrics.

It also provides a priority score for the keyword, reflecting higher volume and lower difficulty.

The tool provides keyword suggestions based on your target keyword and provides monthly search volumes of these relevant keywords.

Ubersuggest

This is a useful tool providing the search volumes of keywords.

In addition to the target keyword, this tool provides relevant long tail versions of that keyword as keyword ideas.

---

[30] https://moz.com/free-seo-tools

The free version reports limited number of these extra keywords, but you can perform new searches and see their search volumes.[31]

The tool assigns a paid difficulty score based on the estimated competition in paid search, and an average cost per click (CPC) level.

Keyword Revealer

This website provides monthly search volume of the target keyword and related keywords.[32]

It provides monthly trends for one year, presents an estimation for the cost per click (CPC) level, and displays a difficulty score.

The free version is limited to three keywords per day.

Which Keywords Should You Use?

It is important to determine the right keywords as they will directly affect your success.

You may organize your keywords based on the following topics:

1. Target Keywords (Topic)

As conversion perspective is important in Google Ads, target keywords should be result-oriented.

The names of your products or product categories (or services and service categories) serve this purpose.

Let's take an ecommerce store selling watches as an example.

---

[31] https://neilpatel.com/ubersuggest/
[32] https://www.keywordrevealer.com

In this site, you may consider using the following keywords and direct people to the category pages they are interested in:

- XYZ Watches (by brand)
- Digital Watches (by type)
- Men's Watches (by audience)
- Titanium Watches (by material)
- Waterproof Watches (by activity / function)

You may also use some additional relevant keywords such as cheap or affordable and direct the people to the category page sorted by the lowest price.

A common mistake is to target a large number of generic keywords in a small number of campaigns.

In this situation, a few keywords will create conversion and other keywords will consume your budget inefficiently.

The people who visit your site with wrong keywords will not generate conversion.

Let's say you are targeting a generic keyword such as "dress" and directing everyone to a page where they see different types of dresses.

When you display all types of dresses in a single category, you cannot match relevant products with the visitors. This will guarantee low conversion.

Instead of this, you should use niche keywords and direct people to subcategories such as party dresses, prom dresses, casual dresses, black dresses, mini dresses, career style, etc.

When your page content matches the perspective of your visitors and you present them exactly what they are looking for, you will enjoy high conversion.

2. Keywords Related to Customer Shopping Journey

After preparing your keyword list using target keywords for an ecommerce store, you will be covering names of your products and categories.

This means that you cover the keywords such as air conditioners or XYZ (brand) 12,000 BTU Air Conditioner.

Now, you can concentrate on the customer shopping journey and add extra keywords to your list that will help you target the consumers at these stages.

You may consider these 4 main stages:

- Awareness (Discovery)
- Research
- Comparison
- Decision (Evaluation and Purchase)

The people in the Awareness stage are at the beginning of their journey and they are not actively looking for products to buy.

They are searching for information about a certain topic or trying to discover solution alternatives to a problem.

For this reason, this is not a priority and you may skip this stage.

If you want to start a long-term relationship, you may focus on keywords such as "house too hot summer" or "house poor insulation" and direct people to your relevant information pages. On those pages you may place links pointing to product pages.

For the Research stage, it is a good idea to match the perspective of consumers.

You may target search queries such as "cabin air conditioner" or "air conditioner size for apartment" and use relevant information pages explaining the topic in a satisfying manner. You can then, display your products, focusing on the features matching the search queries.

For the Comparison stage, you may concentrate on search queries such as "best air conditioner for apartment" or "ABC or XYZ air conditioner", "ABC air conditioner pros cons".

For the Decision stage, you will be targeting consumers who are actively looking for products to buy, so you may target search queries such as "air conditioner prices", "air conditioner online deals" or "air conditioner online shop".

3. Target Audience

Determining target keywords based on products or services is quite straightforward and many people stop at this point.

Concentrating on customer shopping journey provides additional value, but only few ecommerce stores focus on this.

Considering your audience and targeting the keywords that will match the perspective of these people will elevate your project and provide you competitive advantage.

Using this perspective, you may go the extra mile by focusing on target audiences such as college students, men over 40, single women living in big cities, or mothers.

You should create special landing pages on your website for these audiences. On these pages, you should present tailored content for each audience and present relevant products. Once you match their perspective, your will achieve high conversion and enjoy high sales volume.

For a travel brand, in addition to the commonly used location-based keywords such as "Prague vacation", you may use "honeymoon vacation deals", "holiday destinations for single women" or "family vacation destinations".

For a toy brand, you may consider age and gender segmentation such as "toys for 1 year old boys" or "toys for 3 year old girls" This will be more effective and result oriented compared to targeting generic keywords such as "toys".

For a white goods brand, in addition to using product names as standard keywords, you may target keywords such as "dishwasher for single men", "washing machines for baby clothes" or "white goods for the newlywed".

In the previous sections I explained that you can target these specific audiences using Google Ads targeting options.

If you use tailored messages and direct these people to relevant landing pages on your website, you will achieve high conversion.

4. Branded Keywords

Branded keywords are the keywords containing your brand, company, or website name.

As these keywords represent the people who know your brand, branded search queries are highly valuable.

As you cannot focus on campaigns and result oriented sales messages in your search engine optimization project, you should benefit from branded campaigns.

In addition to having a second spot on the search results page, branded campaigns will provide significantly higher conversion than any other campaign.

For this reason, you should focus on branded keywords in a separate campaign.

As this is an important topic, I will elaborate on this in a separate section.

Tips to Refine the Keywords

Choosing the right keywords is important in a Google Ads project. You may get clicks using the wrong keywords, but this will not generate conversion.

When determining the keywords, you may pay attention to the following topics.

Act with the Perspective of Your Audience

Think about your target audience. Which words do these people use to search for your products and services? If you want to bring these people to your website, your point of view has to match their perspective.

This is quite obvious in the hospital websites. Hospitals use keywords such as cardiology or cardiovascular surgery, which is the reflection of their perspective. On the other hand, the people who want to receive service from hospitals do not search with those words. They use the words such as stent or bypass.

In order to be successful in your project, you need to focus on the keywords your target audience uses.

Create a Balance between Generic and Long-tail Keywords

Everyone wants to show their ads for generic keywords. But these keywords have high cost per click, and they are not very result oriented.

For this reason, it is important to pay attention to long-tail keywords as well. These long-tail keywords belong to the people who actually know what they want. For this reason, they usually create higher conversion.

For example, the search volume of "shoes" keyword may be very high, but a large part of this traffic will not generate meaningful conversion. No need to mention, this will consume your budget very quickly.

On the other hand, long-tail searches such as "black leather men's shoes" may be lower in volume, but these searches usually belong to the people who know exactly what they want.

Focus on the Keywords That Will Generate Conversion

When choosing a keyword, it is important to consider the intention of the person performing the search.

Product and service names usually generate good results. Adding words such as best..., which..., ...models, ...prices to these names instead of ...pictures or ...photos will create higher conversion.

Place Emphasis on Divide and Conquer Method

Divide and Conquer method focuses on dividing the audience and presenting each segment tailored content that matches their perspective. This will enable you to use specific keywords on different pages. It will be much more effective than presenting the same content to everyone.

For example, instead of using a generic keyword like "shirt", you can achieve quicker success with niche keywords such as "slim fit shirts", "tuxedo shirts" or "dress shirts".

Improve Your List

Google Ads Keyword Planner and other keyword research tools provide useful information to improve your keyword list.

With a small budget, you can also set up a search campaign using broad match format. This will enable you to see which combinations of these words your target audience uses as well as the search volumes of these words.

When you search for your keywords on Google, relevant keywords are displayed at the bottom of the page. Both from this section and from the section that opens when the search box is clicked, you can see the popular searches on Google.

If it is difficult to decide on similar words, you can use Google Trends to see the comparative search volume of selected keywords.

In this way, you can compare the search volume of -for example- laptop and notebook and see which one is more popular.

Are they the right keywords?

Once you determine your keywords, you need to be sure that these keywords are result oriented.

Will the people visiting your website with these keywords find what they are looking for?

This is important.

Because if they do not, you will experience low conversion and high bounce rate.

You have to make predictions at the initial stage of your ads project. Once the project is implemented, you can examine the results on the Analytics panel and make necessary revisions according to the performance.

Effective Tips for Negative Keywords List

One of the most useful tools to improve the efficiency of keyword targeting is the negative keyword tool.

With this tool, you can create negative keyword lists and add them to your campaigns. If you want, you can also add negative keywords in each campaign or ad group.

If these negative keywords are included in the search query, Google Ads system will not display your ad.

In this way, you will not be wasting money on wrong keywords that will not yield results.

When creating a negative keywords list, you should consider the following keywords:

1. Keywords to Exclude the Users Who Have No Intention to Buy

Some searchers may be using your target keywords, but they may have no intention to buy.

You should exclude these people by adding certain keywords to your negative keywords list.

Based on the nature of your product or service, you may consider the following keywords:

Job

career, careers, curriculum vitae, CV, employer, employers, employment, full time, hire, hiring, intern, interns, internship, internships, job, job opening, job openings, jobs, looking for work, new hires, occupation, occupations, opening, openings, opportunities, opportunity, part time, recruiter, recruiters, recruiting, recruitment, resume, resumes, salaries, salary, work, etc.

Research

about, article, articles, association, associations, book, books, calculator, case studies, case study, data, define, definition, diagram, example, examples, forum, forums, guide, guides, history, journal, journals, learn about, magazine, magazines, map, maps, measurement, metrics, news, newspaper, pdf, quote, quotes, report, reports, research, resource, resources, review, reviews, rule, rules, sample, samples, specifications, statistics, stats, success stories, success story, tip, tips, what, when, white paper, white papers, etc.

Education

certification, certifications, class, classes, club, clubs, college, colleges, conference, conferences, council, councils, course, courses, education, exam, exams, institute, institutes, instructor, instructors, program, programs, school, schools, seminar, seminars, teacher, teachers, textbook, textbooks, training, tutor, tutorial, tutorials, tutors, universities, university, workshop, workshops, etc.

Do it yourself

craft, crafts, create, creating, DIY, do it yourself, hand made, handmade, home, homemade, how can, how can I, how do I, how does, how to, make, making, etc.

Purpose

advisory, client relation, client relations, client relationship, complaint, complaints, consultant, consultants, consulting, customer relation, customer relations, customer relationship, how to fix, how to repair, law, laws, legal, legislation, logo, logos, maintenance, regulation, regulations, rent, rental, repair, repairing, service, toy, toys, used, etc.

2. Keywords to Exclude the Users Who Are Not in Your Target Audience

Budget (especially if you are selling premium products)

bargain, cheap, cheapest, clearance, close out, close outs, close-out, closeouts, discount, discounted, discounts, free, free sample, freeware, hack, hacks, inexpensive, liquidation, low cost, outlet, overstock, remainder, remainders, etc.

Gender

child, children, children's, girl, girls, lady, ladies, woman, women, women's, etc. (for keywords such as suit, shirt, jacket for a men's clothing brand) (and vice versa).

Trade

export, exporter, exporters, import, importer, importers, merchandise, trade

Brand

If you think that the customers of certain brands do not match your target audience, you may consider adding them as negative keywords.

This way if someone searches for XYZ refrigerator using their brand name, your ad will not be displayed.

3. Keywords That Do Not Match Product Specifications

Material

aluminum, ceramic, cotton, fabric, glass, gold, iron, leather, metal, paper, plastic, rubber, silver, stainless steel, steel, stone, vinyl, wood, etc.

Color

black, blue, brown, cerulean, gray, green, indigo, orange, red, scarlet, violet, white, yellow, etc.

Language

bengali, chinese, english, french, german, hindi, italian, japanese, korean, portuguese, russian, spanish, turkish, urdu, etc.

Country / Region / City

argentina, australia, brazil, canada, china, france, germany, india, italy, japan, mexico, russia, turkey, united kingdom, united states, etc.

Product specifications

evening dress, evening dresses, party dress, party dresses, etc. (if you are selling casual clothes); denim, jeans, etc. (if you are selling formal trousers).

4. Irrelevant Keywords

Multimedia

film, films, gif, gifs, graphic, graphics, icon, icons, image, images, jpeg, jpegs, jpg, lyric, lyrics, movie, movies, music, music video, photo, photograph, photographs, photos, picture, pictures, pics, pix, png, pngs, ringtones, video, videos, etc.

Social media

blog, blogs, face book, facebook, instagram, linkedin, pinterest, slideshare, snapchat, tik tok, tiktok, twitter, vine, youtube, utube, etc.

Even if you prepared your negative keyword list and applied it to your campaigns, there might still be some keywords you have missed out.

Therefore, you should always check the keywords in the Google Ads search terms section.

As irrelevant keywords emerge, you should add them to your list.

What Determines the Quality Score? How Can You Get the Highest Quality Score?

The Google Ads system functions based on a quality score.

Google sets a quality score from 1 to 10 for each keyword to ensure a good user experience. 1 is the lowest score and 10 is the highest.

Google encourages showing the right ads to the right people.

Ads having high quality scores enjoy lower cost per click and higher ad position, while ads having very low quality scores are not displayed.

Google Ads system assigns a quality score to the keywords in your ad group. Each keyword has its own quality score.

You can see the quality score of your keywords by selecting campaign > ad groups > keywords.

If you do not see "Quality Score" as a column, you may select Modify Columns and add this option to your dashboard.

As the performance data is required to calculate the quality score, it may change over time based on performance.

3 topics determine the quality score:

1. Ad Click Through Rate (CTR)

Similar to SEO results, Google knows the average click through rate of every rank in the Google Ads system.

If the click through rate of your ad is higher than the average rate of that rank, observing the positive interest of people, Google will assign you a higher quality score.

Based on the campaign structure, target segments, target keywords or ad content, the average click through rate of Google search ads may range from 2% to 8%.

When you communicate with niche audiences and use tailored messages that will motivate them the most, you can achieve a higher click through rate than the average.

The click through rate of your ads can reach 35% to 45% for branded terms. Together with ad relevance and landing page experience, this usually results in 10/10 quality score.

Based on the click performance of your ad, Google assigns your ad one of these three statuses: above average, average, or below average.

Obviously, above average status contributes to your quality score the most, whereas you do not get any points for below average status.

Therefore, you should monitor the performance of your keywords closely and revise or remove low performing keywords.

2. Ad Relevance

Google attaches importance to ad relevance.

Your ad content should be relevant to the search query in order to get a high quality score.

If the keywords used in the search query are also used in your ad content (especially in the headline section), this will provide a high ad relevance.

Creating tailored ad groups for specific keyword groups and using relevant content in each of them will provide the best result.

This will also help you to achieve a higher click through rate.

Same as the click through rate, Google ads system assigns one of the above average, average, or below average statuses.

If your ad content is highly relevant to the keyword, you get above average status.

If your ad is assigned a below average status, you may try to rewrite the ad content. You may be addressing the topic too broadly and might not be using enough keywords.

3. Landing Page Relevance and User Experience

With every ad, you direct people to your webpages. The relevance and usability of these webpages also affect the quality score.

Your ad content may be relevant to the search query and you may have a high click through rate, but Google also wants to be sure that it does not direct people to a webpage where they will have a bad experience.

The landing page experience status represents the experience of visitors who click on your ad and come to your webpage.

Based on this, Google system assigns one of the above average, average, or below average statuses.

To get the best result, your website must have a good usability and your webpage content should be relevant to the search query and ad content.

You should provide relevant, clear and useful content to visitors.

You should be specific and present what the customers are searching for. If they are searching for party dresses, they should be seeing party dresses, not all kinds of different dresses.

If you are asking the visitors to submit information you should be clear on how you will be using that information.

You should not hide your company name and your contact information.

You should not automatically redirect visitors to other webpages.

Taking all this into account, it is clear that you should not direct people to your home page, you should direct everyone to a relevant landing page.

As Google attaches importance to site speed you should make sure that your pages are loading fast.

Having a mobile friendly website and high mobile user experience (UX) also contribute to the success of landing page status.

Calculation

A study by AdAlysis revealed the calculation of the quality score.[33]

See the table on the next page:

---

[33] https://searchengineland.com/reverse-engineering-adwords-quality-score-factors-244192

	Landing Page Experience	Ad Relevance	Click Through Rate
Above average	3.5	2	3.5
Average	1.75	1	1.75
Below average	0	0	0

They stated the formula as: **1 + Landing Page Experience weight + Ad Relevance weight + CTR weight**.

This suggests that the landing page experience and click through rate have higher weight than ad relevance.

In other words, no matter what you write in your ad content, your quality score will be 3 at most, if your click through rate and landing page experience are below average.

Conclusion

When you achieve the best performance in these three topics, you pay a lower price for clicks and the rank of your ad improves.

You can feel this advantage clearly for ads having 8/10 or higher scores.

Google decreases the impression of (and sometimes even does not show) ads having 3/10 or lower scores.

This indicates that adding high number of different keywords into the same ad group is really a bad idea. Irrelevant keywords will reduce your quality score and make your campaign inefficient.

To achieve the best performance, you should segment your target audience, create tailored campaigns for each segment and use niche keywords in each campaign.

When you direct the users to the relevant landing pages on your website, you can achieve the highest quality score.

How Can You Write the Ad Content Effectively?

Google search ads have much more features today, compared to a few years ago.

Google Ads system increased the number of the fields used in search ads. Together with ad extensions, you may now use various topics in a single ad content.

Headlines

As the headline of the ad is displayed using a larger font and in blue color (similar to an organic search result), people are most likely to notice the headline of the ad first.

For this reason, you should give importance to this and present your main campaign message here.

To achieve the best performance, you should think like your target audience and try to use the keywords they use in search queries.

The text ad consists of three headlines where you can enter up to 30 characters each.

The headlines are separated by a vertical pipe ("|") and may show differently based on different devices.

Using the first headline as "ABC (your brand name) Online Store" produces good result for branded campaigns. As people are familiar with your brand, they should see your brand name.

For other campaigns you may use your brand name together with keywords, such as ABC Plus Size Dress.

Regarding the ads aiming to promote your products and services, you should use relevant product and product category names as keywords to achieve high ad relevance.

You should emphasize your advantages and motivate the target audience to achieve high click through rate.

As the Google Ads system does not always display the third headline, the main focus should be on the first two headlines.

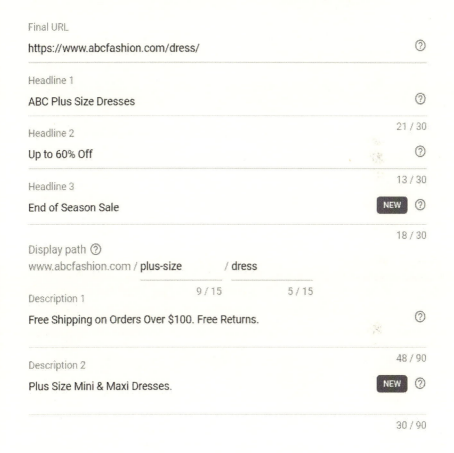

Including a call to action in the ad content often increases click through rate. You may use words such as "Get, Buy, Shop, Try, Discover".

It is a good idea to include special offers like "Up to 60% Off". It will be much more effective than using a standard message such as "Browse Our Collection".

You may provide numbers to motivate your audience. You may highlight the number of your members, customers, stores. You may talk about awards to build trust.

This is not a rule, but you may focus on an emotional perspective for women and a rational perspective for men.

You should be specific and match the searcher's perspective in your ad content.

Remember that the people encounter with hundreds of messages every day, they glance over the content, they do not read thoroughly.

If the searcher is looking for a laptop, he/she should see laptop keyword in your ad content.

To achieve this, you should create different ad groups for different group of keywords.

Display URL & Final URL

The display URL shows your website address.

This URL displays your domain name and two optional "Path" fields, each having 15-character limit.

The text in path fields does not have to match the exact URL of the landing pages.

The display URL gives potential customers a clear idea of what webpage they will reach once they click your ad, so your path text should describe your ad's landing page.

For this reason, you may use keywords in the display path even if the final URL is different.

You may leave this area empty for branded campaigns and add relevant keywords for other campaigns.

The final URL is the URL that people reach after clicking your ad.

It should match what your ad promotes. If you target "laptop" keyword and use "laptop" in the headline of the ad, you should direct the users to a page where they see laptops. Directing them to a page where there are different types of computers will only result in spending your money and not getting any results.

Description

There are two description fields in Google search ads.

Within a 90-character limit, you may highlight details about your product or service.

You may talk about your advantages (such as free returns or global delivery) and motivate your target segment.

It is a good idea to use relevant keywords in these fields.

Even though the limit is 90 characters, it is better to keep your content shorter.

If you did not use call to action words in the headline section, you may use them here. As you want the users to take a specific action, you should make that action clear.

This may reduce the click through rate a little but as the searchers who click on the ad will be coming to your website knowingly and willingly, it will increase your conversion.

Content & Click Through Rate

In the previous section, I explained that the click through rate has more weight in quality score than ad relevance.

Therefore, in addition to using relevant keywords in your ad content, you should also write the ad content effectively to motivate the target segment to click.

This will enhance your overall ad quality score.

Content & Landing Page

Landing page experience also significantly affects the quality score. Using the search terms in your landing page will provide consistency and will assure the visitors that they are on the right page.

For this reason, it is important to direct every visitor to a relevant landing page on your website.

Directing everyone to your home page will cause below average landing page experience and lower your quality score.

Although this is the case, a study found that 98% of 300 different landing pages did not correctly align the ad message match.[34]

You can increase both your quality score and your conversion by acting differently.

Other Tips

For the system to function efficiently you should write more than one ad content. If possible, you may use at least three ads.

You might focus on different aspects or slightly change the original content and focus on the same topic.

Google system will use these ads interchangeably and make a decision based on the performance.

This will also enable you to understand the click preferences of your audience.

---

[34] https://unbounce.com/ppc/poor-message-match/

How Can You Use the Ad Extensions Effectively?

The Google Ads system allows you to enrich your ad using ad extensions.

With these extensions, you can make your ad more effective and result oriented.

Ad extensions also improve the quality score by increasing the ad relevance and the click through rate.

Google stated that the ad extensions and formats can influence the position of the ad on the search results page.[35]

As your ad will occupy more space in search results page with ad extensions, this may lead to more clicks.

Google stated in another article that implementing extensions is often an immediate and highly impactful way to improve click through rate and there may be 10-15% click through rate uplift from implementing a new ad extension.[36]

Ad extensions are completely free to use. You do not need to pay an additional fee, or your cost per click will not increase.

As you can add different aspects to your ad, you can make it more efficient and powerful.

Ad extensions may be used at the account level, campaign level or ad group level.

From the Google Ads main menu, you may select Ads & Extensions > Extensions to see active extensions and to create new ones.

Let's take a look at how you can use them effectively:

---

[35] https://adwords.googleblog.com/2013/10/improving-ad-rank.html
[36] https://support.google.com/google-ads/answer/6167131

Sitelink Extensions

As sitelink extensions are very easy to use and they provide significant value, they are heavily used by the advertisers.

Using this extension, you can provide links to different pages on your website from a single ad. You can direct everyone to the specific pages that they are interested in.

For example, for an ad targeting your skin creams page, you may use ad extensions for subcategories such as hand creams, eye creams, and anti-aging creams. You may also create a site extension for your sign-up page.

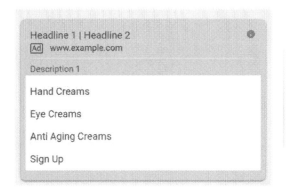

A sitelink extension is composed of a sitelink text and a description line.

Sitelink text is the clickable area and has a limit of 25 characters. You may use this area as the headline.

Description line has a limit of 35 characters. You may use additional explanations in this area.

As the Google Ads systems offers you to use two lines as the description line, it helps to extend the ad area on Google search results page.

It is a good idea to use this to occupy more space.

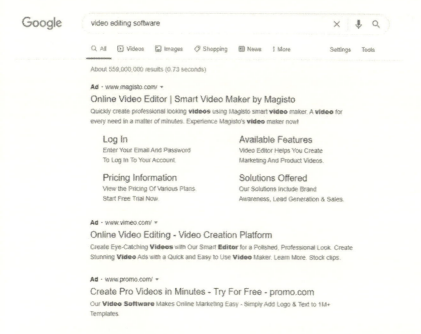

If possible, you should use 3 to 5 site extensions. Google Ads system will display them interchangeably and measure their performance.

Callout Extensions

Callout extensions are also widely used. You simply write some additional text as an extension.

This enables you to extend your ad copy, talk about important topics, and highlight your business offerings such as "free returns, free shipping, 24/7 support, or global delivery" without restricting yourself to the character limit of the ad content.

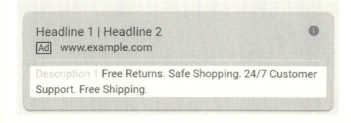

There is 25-character limit to callout extensions, but it is better to keep them shorter.

You may complement the ad copy, highlight additional aspects, or emphasize your strengths.

It is a good idea to customize the callout extension for each campaign. For example, if you have a mobile only campaign you may focus on mobile features.

If possible, you should use 3 to 5 callout extensions. Google system will display them interchangeably and measure their performance.

Location Extensions

Location extensions help people find your locations by showing your ads with your address, a map to your location, or the distance to your business.

Location extensions may also include a phone number or call button so that users can easily call your business.

If your business operates in a physical location or has stores in multiple locations, you can benefit from location extensions.

You can also enter specific chain locations where your products are sold.

Using this feature, you can help especially mobile searchers to find your physical locations easily.

In an article, Google presented information about how the mobile search connects customers to stores.[37]

The article stated that there was an increase in mobile searches for the terms "stores open now", or "where to buy/find/get".

---

[37] https://www.thinkwithgoogle.com/consumer-insights/mobile-search-trends-consumers-to-stores/

The article also stated that 76% of people who searched on their smartphones for something nearby, visited that company's business within a day. 28% of those searchers purchased a product.

Location extensions need Google My Business to work.

To use location extensions, you may select curated locations or link to a Google My Business account.

Clicking on the location extension will be counted as a click, but this does not direct the visitor to the website. Instead, it directs the user to Google Maps entry.

You may also publish ads on Google Maps in addition to using location extension in search campaigns.

I will elaborate on Local Search Ads in a different section.

Call Extensions

Call extensions let you add phone numbers to your ads and enable the searchers to call your business by simply clicking on the extension.

If you attempt to include a phone number elsewhere in your ad text, it may lead to the disapproval of the ad. So, if you would like to include a phone number, it is best to use a call extension.

Call extensions may be displayed as clickable buttons on mobile devices, and this makes it easy for people to call you directly from their phones with a single click.

This has significant importance for local businesses.

As the conversion they are looking for is the phone calls, they can achieve this directly from the ad.

Ecommerce stores and other brands may also use their support lines in this section, but this will increase their workload.

If you are using this extension, you should make sure that someone answers the phone when the ads are running.

A company selling glass products was trying to reach distributors in selected countries. They had a sales representative for each country, and they were using their phone numbers as call extensions in ads targeting those countries.

They achieved significantly more conversion compared to directing everyone to the website and waiting for them to find the phone number in the contact page.

In addition to using call extensions, you can also create call-only campaigns. I will elaborate on this in a different section.

Structured Snippet Extensions

Structured snippets enable you to provide additional information regarding your business.

You can highlight specific aspects of your products and services with structured snippets extensions.

Structured snippets show beneath your text ad in the form of a header (ex: "Destinations") and list of values (ex: "Mexico, Brazil, Uruguay").

Structured snippets give visitors a preview of the nature and range of your products and services, before they click on your ad.

Google Ads systems presents these options:

Amenities, Brands, Courses, Degree Programs, Destinations, Featured Hotels, Insurance Coverage, Models, Neighborhoods, Service Catalog, Shows, Styles, Types.

You can list at least 3 features, services, or products related to the selected option.

Each item is limited to 25 characters.

Price Extensions

The price of a product or service is a significant factor in decision making.

Using price extensions, you can make the price clear for the potential customers.

Some people may decide not to click on the ad when they see the price, and this will naturally reduce your click through rate. But this will increase your conversion rate as the people coming to your website will be knowing the price and they are still interested.

It is a good idea to test the performance of this extension.

If the result shows that you can convince the visitors on your website before they see the price, you do not need to use this extension. If people still do not buy when they see the price you may use this extension to eliminate those people.

Google Ads system presents these options:

Brands, Events, Locations, Neighborhoods, Product Categories, Product Tiers, Service Categories, Service Tiers, Services.

You may benefit from price extensions regarding event tickets, hotel rooms, vacation packages, hair salon services, or any other product or service.

You can use price qualifiers such as from, up to, or average. This will enable you to use the price as "from $9.99".

Google Ads system requires you to enter at least 3 items.

App Extensions

If you have a mobile application, you can benefit from app extensions.

App extensions allow you to provide a link to your mobile app from your ads.

People may still click on your ad headline to go to your website.

When they click on this extension, they will be directed to a relevant app store, directing to your app. They will not be coming to your website.

This means that you can provide access both to your website and to your app from a single ad.

When creating an app extension, you can select your mobile app's platform as iOS or Android.

Google Ads system will display this extension using "Download Now" message.

Promotion Extensions

Promotions provide an important motivation to drive sales. You can mention a promotion in your ad headline or description, you can also use promotion extensions.

Promotion extensions make your offer stand out so potential customers can spot deals easily.

This feature may be helpful to distinguish your ad among others, especially during holiday and seasonal sales campaigns.

Google Ads system allows you to select the "Occasion" to include a holiday or special event for your promotion. Each occasion is eligible to show during select dates.

The occasion options are Back to school, Black Friday, Boxing Day, Carnival, Chinese New Year, Christmas, Cyber Monday, Diwali, Easter, Eid al-Adha, Eid al-Fitr, End of Season, Epiphany, Fall Sale, Father's Day, Halloween, Hanukkah, Holi, Independence Day, Labor Day, Mother's Day, National Day, Navratri, New Year's, Parent's Day, Passover, Ramadan, Rosh Hashanah, Singles

Day, Spring Sale, St. Nicholas Day, Summer Sale, Valentine's Day, Winter Sale, and Women's Day.

If you select a special occasion it is displayed as a bold label next to your promotional text.

Lead Form Extensions

Lead form extensions help you to capture interest when potential customers are searching for your company, products, or services on Google.

You can use a call to action such as Learn More, Get Quote, Apply Now, Sign Up, Contact Us, Subscribe, Download, Book Now, or Get Offer and write an extension text.

You can then create a lead form to get data from the users.

Although the users will not be coming to your website, this is a faster and easier way to collect data.

Using Audiences in Search Ads

I explained the types of audiences in the previous chapter. In this section I will focus on the strategies for the search ads.

Especially when you are targeting generic keywords, using audience targeting will be very beneficial to refine your target audience and to increase your conversion.

As generic keywords have high search volume and they usually require high cost per click, you will be targeting a wide audience and you will be spending your budget very quickly.

When you use audience targeting you can overcome this inefficiency. You can use demographics and detailed demographics to identify the audience, affinity categories to refine their interests, in-market segments to focus on conversion.

Using audiences in search ads will enable you to achieve high conversion by using tailored messages when communicating with your target segments.

For example, for a cosmetics brand, you may select in-market > beauty > anti-aging segment and use a tailored message to influence the decision of these people who are in the market to buy anti-aging products. You may select 45+ years old women living in big cities to further refine this segment.

For a men's fashion brand, you may select in-market > apparel > formal wear > suits. As generic keywords such as suits have high cost per click, it will be a good idea to target this segment to use your budget wisely. You may select 35+ years old men, in business districts, at noon or during working hours to further refine this segment.

If you sell premium products and your prices are higher than your competitors, you may select affinity > shoppers > luxury shoppers. You may try to further refine this segment by selecting high household income, specific devices, or high-income districts.

You can use remarketing audiences to target people who are familiar with your brand and similar audiences to reach new users who may be more interested in your message compared to cold audiences.

Google Ads system allows you to differentiate your CPC bid for different target audiences. You may allocate a special budget for selected target audiences, or you can increase your bids for warm audiences.

For example, you can set higher cost per click for those who have visited your website. This way, you can rank your ad higher when these people search for relevant keywords on Google. It usually produces higher conversion.

I will talk more about targeting audiences in the display ads chapter, after I elaborate on targeting options.

How Can You Benefit from Auction Insights?

Google Ads system presents auction insights report for search and shopping campaigns. You may select Ad Groups > Auction Insights to see your performance.

This report enables you to see which advertisers you are competing against and lets you compare your performance with other advertisers who are participating in the same auctions that you are.

This information can help you make decisions about bidding and budgeting, by showing you where you are succeeding and where you may be missing opportunities.

The report provides information about competing domains, impression share, overlap rate, position above rate, top of page rate, absolute top of page rate, and outranking share.

Impression share is the number of impressions you received divided by the estimated number of impressions you were eligible to receive.

Overlap rate is how often another participant's ad received an impression when your ad also received an impression.

Position above rate is how often the other participant's ad was shown in a higher position than your ad.

Top of page rate tells you how often your ad was shown above the unpaid search results.

Absolute top of the page rate tells you how often your ad was shown as the very first ad above the organic search results.

Outranking share is calculated as the number of times your ad ranked higher in the auction than another participant's ad, plus the number of times your ad showed when theirs did not, divided by the total number of ad auctions you participated in.

Depending on who your competitors are, you can explore efficient niche areas and focus on opportunities.

If your competitors are very strong such as amazon.com there is no point in trying to rank at the absolute top of the page. Top of page rate performance will be satisfactory.

If you are competing against such powerful websites, you may work on your ad content to differentiate your message.

When all of the ads say the same thing, the users may tend to click on the ads of well-known, powerful websites.

Since this system has a dynamic nature and all advertisers can make changes at any time, you should constantly monitor the competition and make changes accordingly.

Branded Campaign Strategies

Your website probably ranks on top of the search results page as the first organic result regarding search queries including your company or brand name.

For this reason, many companies think that there is no need to use Google search ads for branded terms.

As the organic search results for branded terms display the text used in page title and meta description, they are organized for SEO purposes. They are not suitable for result-oriented short-term marketing messages such as campaign announcements.

On the other hand, people who perform branded searches are familiar with your brand and they are the users who will create the best conversion.

Therefore, using branded ads you can promote your current campaigns to these people and direct them to specific landing pages on your website.

If you are worried about cannibalization, you may measure your results with and without branded ads.

In almost all of the cases, organic results and branded ads together produce more traffic and more conversion than only the organic results.

Two factors contribute to this result.

The ad content usually provides more motivation, increasing the click through rate in search results page.

Also, as you have an additional listing on the search results page, other organic search results will be displayed further down on the page and you will be taking at least some of the click share of those results.

Branded ads help you to dominate the search engine results page by having a spot on the top of the page, above all other results.

By using ad extensions, you will be occupying a pretty big area at the top. In a way, you will be having a customizable area for your branded terms to deliver your message.

As you can see on the next page, branded ads occupy a significant area on the search results page. This enables the brands to achieve the best result from their audience.

As branded terms are highly relevant and they have high click through rate, the quality score is generally 10/10.

This means that the cost per click will be low. As this is warm audience the conversion will be high, and this will allow you to achieve impressive results at low cost.

This type of advertising may generate around 10 to 40 dollars ecommerce sales for each 1 dollar spent.

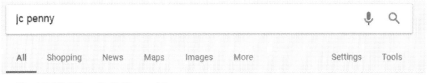

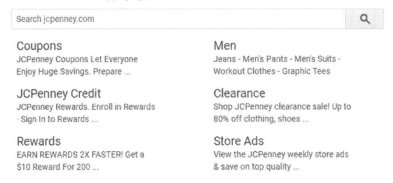

If you do not use branded ad campaigns and if your competitors or other websites selling your products use them, you will be losing your customers to other sites. You should protect your brand and fight for your own customers.

To see which websites are bidding for your branded keywords, you may use Auction Insights.

A common mistake in branded ads is to use the brand name in broad match format and direct all the visitors to home page using a single ad content.

When you use your brand name in broad match format, your ad will also be displayed for the searches performed with various keywords other than your brand name.

As Google Ads system determines which keywords are relevant to your brand name, it may display your ad for irrelevant or unproductive generic search terms.

For example, an ad for a fashion brand may be displayed for search terms such as women's dress or evening dresses in addition to the brand name.

This format will quickly consume your budget and lead to an inefficient branded campaign.

Your brand or website name should be the main keyword. To achieve the best performance, it is a good idea to add extra target keywords in addition to your brand name.

This will enable you to direct each audience to relevant webpages using different ad groups.

You can direct the users searching for your brand name to your main campaign page.

For the search queries including your brand name and product category name, you can direct people to the relevant category pages.

If people are using your brand name and discount keyword as the search query, you can direct them to your outlet page (or your collection page sorted by discount rate).

For example, for a fashion brand you may use a structure such as:

Search query		Directed to
ABC, ABC fashion	>>>	current campaign page
ABC dress	>>>	dress category page
ABC cheap dress	>>>	dress category page sorted by price
ABC discount, outlet	>>>	outlet page or collection page sorted by discount rate

Directing everyone to a relevant page with a single click will provide a good landing page experience and high conversion rate.

Product (& Service) Campaign Strategies

Before starting to work on products, it is important to determine which products or product categories you will target in your campaigns.

In the "What Is the Value of Google Ads Campaigns?" section and "Scope of the Google Ads Project" chapter, I explained that some product groups might not produce feasible results.

After this stage, you may create different ad campaigns for product categories and focus on relevant keywords.

In the "Which Keywords Should You Use?" section, I explained four topics to choose the right keywords.

In this section, I will provide an example based on those topics.

Let's say you are managing Google Ads campaigns for an ecommerce store selling refrigerators.

Regarding target keywords, every brand wants to target generic keywords such as refrigerator.

However, these generic keywords often have very high cost per click and they produce low conversion because the terms are very broad.

In order not to consume your budget too fast and inefficiently, you may lower the cost per click or refine the ad settings, targeting the right audience.

For a better performance, you may use category names such as french door refrigerators, side-by-side refrigerators, bottom freezer refrigerators, top freezer refrigerators.

(Note: I am providing the following keywords only to use as examples. You now know that you will not use them in broad match format.)

The common mistake is to use a single ad group and place all of these keywords in this same ad group.

To achieve the best performance, you should create separate ad groups for these categories and direct the users to relevant pages on your website.

You may add keywords such as "service" or "care" to the negative keyword list or you may test the performance of a message such as "If you are tired of frequently calling the service, change your refrigerator.".

Regarding keywords related to customer shopping journey, you may skip the awareness stage because it will not be result-oriented.

For the Research stage, you may target keywords such as "which refrigerator for summer house", or "2021 refrigerator models".

For the Comparison stage, you may concentrate on search queries such as "ABC or XYZ refrigerator", "ABC refrigerator pros cons", "refrigerator reviews", "refrigerator comparison", "best refrigerator", "competitor brand name + refrigerator". You may emphasize the comparative advantages of your products.

For the Decision stage, you may target keywords such as "refrigerator prices", "refrigerator online deals" "buy refrigerator" or "refrigerator online shopping". You may direct the users to your campaign pages.

Regarding keywords related to your target audience, you may focus on search queries such as "refrigerator models for the newlywed", "eco-friendly refrigerator", "refrigerator models for single men".

You should also target branded keywords to defend your territory.

You can improve your conversion in product campaigns by segmenting your audience and communicating with each segment using tailored messages.

For a premium home textile brand (selling high quality but expensive products), you may focus on only the prestigious regions in metropolises and target high-income users. For baby products, you may target mothers who visited that category on your website. You may use tailored messages for bamboo products, targeting the people who give importance to naturalness.

For a cafe, you may select a specific area on the map with a pin. You may communicate with the business professionals and deliver your message about lunch before noon and about happy hour in the afternoon.

For a residential project, you may communicate with 25-54 years old, high income, university graduate people working in a commercial district close to your project. You may communicate with them during the daytime, focusing on the benefits of living close to the workplace.

To attract international customers to your hotel, you may communicate with them in their own language. Based on demographic and psychographic segmentation, you may emphasize different topics such as history, shopping, or nature.

You have a great power to target the right people and communicate the right message at the right time. You should use it.

A men's clothing brand was targeting all the men in the entire country with their product ads.

When they segmented their target audience and formulated tailored suggestions for each segment such as office style (with ads during working hours in the selected regions of metropolises), slim fit shirts (for young age group) and classic fit shirts (for middle age group), they increased their conversion significantly.

A dairy brand targeted middle age women living in big cities and interested in healthy lifestyle for low-fat milk product, and middle and upper age women interested in nutritional supplements for calcium-enriched milk product.

After using tailored messages, they received positive feedback from each segment. They retargeted the people who visited the specific product pages on their website and continued the communication with banner ads.

To achieve the best performance and to use your budget efficiently, you should make sure that you identified the right products or product categories, segmented your audience correctly, and formulated tailored messages for each segment.

A tele-sales representative who did not know about my profession called me a long time ago.

She was telling me that my site would be displayed on the first page of Google for any keyword I want, for a monthly fee of only 30 dollars.

I let her continue. I said, "I want to appear on top for many generic keywords such as book, computer, mobile phone, etc. for 1 dollar per day", to which she said, "Of course sir, we will ensure that your site ranks high for any keyword you wish".

Then I said "Ok, but how will you be able to do this for these expensive keywords?" to which she said, "We have a great team, they will handle it".

This may be the level you encounter in the market.

Dynamic Search Ads

Dynamic Search Ads enable you to reach the users searching on Google for precisely what you offer.

When Google crawls your website, it determines the relevant keywords for each page.

When a user performs a search on Google using search terms closely related to the titles and phrases on your website, Google Ads system will use these titles and phrases to select a landing page and generate a relevant headline for your ad.

As the system automatically targets the keywords even having low search volume, it increases the keyword coverage and enables you to observe the performance of these keywords.

As Dynamic Search Ad headlines and landing pages are generated using content from your website, all you need to do is to add a creative description.

The attractive aspect of this campaign type is to target all of your pages to generate conversion.

This campaign type yields good results for ecommerce stores where product name and description fields are well-organized. For example, you can offer a tailored suggestion to the people who are searching for "Round Neck Long Sleeve Blouse".

When using this model, you should organize your pages considering the possible search queries of your target audience. You should focus on page titles and the headlines in your page content.

As your website is automatically targeted, dynamic ads may be displayed for some irrelevant keywords. For this reason, it is important to monitor these campaigns closely.

You should monitor the search terms continuously, and in addition to your standard negative keywords list, you should add irrelevant keywords to your campaign.

GOOGLE DISPLAY ADS

The two main advantages of Google display ads compared to search ads are being able to communicate your message visually and reaching your target audience on Google Display Network.

You should keep in mind that many websites that cannot generate revenue, place Google Ads ad slots on their pages to earn revenue. Most of them are low-quality sites that produce no valuable content. If your ads are published on these websites, they will not generate conversion.

Therefore, you should be very careful when targeting the audiences and the websites in display ad campaigns.

To get rid of these websites and to achieve high conversion, you should exclude certain placements at the account level.

As you will probably have various display campaigns, it will be much more difficult to apply this to the campaigns one by one.

You should select Placements > Exclusions from Google Ads menu to reach this page.

Google Ads system displays five options as Websites, YouTube channels, YouTube videos, Apps, and App categories.

For the first four options, you may search and select placements to exclude, or manually enter the URLs.

For example, you may select Websites and search for games keyword. When the Google Ads system lists you the game websites you may select and exclude them all.

As excluding YouTube channels and videos manually is almost impossible, you may select Websites option, search for YouTube keyword and exclude the domain there, if you do not want your ads to be displayed on YouTube.

For App categories, you can select and exclude categories from a list. App targeting is usually very inefficient and will consume your budget quickly without producing any results.

In total, there are more than 140 App categories.

Unfortunately, Google Ads system does not have a single button to select and exclude all App categories.

So, unless you have a reason to act otherwise, you should select them one by one and close them all.

You should be careful not to miss the subcategories.

For example, regarding some categories such as games, you can only see the main category name and selecting that name does not automatically select the subcategories.

For this reason, you should click on the main category name to open the secondary pull-down menu, where you see the subcategories. There, you should select all of them.

This is account level exclusion.

You may also exclude placements at campaign level or ad group level.

For example, there is also game category under Topics menu. As you cannot exclude Topics at the account level, you have to do it at the campaign level.

Excluding websites may take some time, but it is necessary if you want to achieve high conversion.

For certain campaigns, you may want to target specific App placements or categories.

For example, regarding financial products you may want to target Investing App.

In such a situation, you should deselect the relevant category in the exclusion list and add that App to targeting list.

You may exclude that category for other display campaigns, at the campaign level.

Remarketing Ads

The Power of Remarketing

Google Ads system tags the users visiting your website and displays remarketing ads to these people on display network.

Remarketing ads enable you to continue communicating with the people who visited your website and who are familiar with your brand.

These people might also visit the websites of competitor brands. Using remarketing ads, you make sure that these people do not forget about your brand.

A study on Moz blog states that ecommerce sites have an average conversion rate of 1.6%.[38]

Criteo says only 4% of site visitors end up making a purchase.[39]

This means that although you work hard and probably use a significant budget to get visitors to your website, 96% - 98% of your visitors will leave your website without making a purchase.

---

[38] https://moz.com/blog/ecommerce-benchmark-kpi-study-2017
[39] https://www.criteo.com/what-is-retargeting/

As these people are familiar with your brand and products, they are more likely to buy compared to cold audiences, and you should continue communicating with them to achieve conversion.

As you target a warm audience, the click through rate is usually above 1% (significantly above than standard display campaigns).

The conversion rate is also usually higher than standard display campaigns.

For this reason, marketers give priority to remarketing ads.

A report on IAB website states that 71% of marketers spend 10–50% of their entire online ad budget on retargeting. Over 90% of marketers report that retargeting performs as well as or better than search, email, and other display campaigns.[40]

Segment Your Audience

Identifying all of your website visitors as a single target audience and directing everybody to your home page using a single marketing message will not produce a high conversion.

You may do this by directing the people to your campaign pages when you announce some major campaigns.

However, the strategy that will ensure the highest conversion is to segment the people visiting your website and deliver relevant messages to each segment.

How can you perform this segmentation?

You can group people who visit a certain page or group of pages on your site.

For a fashion site, it is a good idea to segment people who visited men's and women's categories, people who visited a specific cat-

---

[40] https://www.iab.com/wp-content/uploads/2015/07/US_AdRoll_State_of_the_Industry.pdf

egory page such as prom dresses, price-oriented people who visited outlet page, people who visited shopping cart page, etc.

When you communicate with each segment using the most relevant message, you will achieve the highest conversion.

You can segment the people who live in a certain country, city or region. You can target or exclude the groups to which your ads will be displayed, based on age, gender, parental status and household income. You can target selected videos on YouTube.

For a hotel, you may communicate with your visitors from different regions in their own languages. You may segment people according to their interests and use different visuals having different themes such as shopping, history or nature.

For a cosmetics brand, you may target mothers who visit the baby cosmetics page on your site. You may further refine this group by selecting metropolises.

Ads

For a long time, Google required advertisers to upload fixed-size banners to its system and matched these banners with ad slots on the display network.

Although this is still an option, more emphasis is placed on responsive ad format which automatically adjusts its size, appearance, and format to fit all available ad spaces. This boosts efficiency for Google.

To create a responsive ad, you upload your assets (images, headlines, logos, videos, and descriptions), and Google automatically generates ads to be shown on the Google Display Network.

The brands having strong visuals (such as fashion brands) may still consider using fixed-size banners to have more control over the visual.

If you prefer to use fixed-size banners, you should use them in a separate ad group. If you place them in the same ad group together with a responsive ad, the responsive ad will probably get almost all of the impressions and consume the budget.

As images affect the performance directly, you should try to use effective, powerful images.

Responsive ads let you upload up to 15 images in two aspect ratios: 1.91:1 for landscape and 1:1 for square. You may also upload up to 5 videos.

Responsive ads enable you to benefit from the power of search ads on Google Display Network, as they allow you to write up to 5 headlines, a long headline, and up to 5 descriptions.

The headline is the first line of your ad and can be up to 30 characters.

The description adds to the headline and provides additional context or details. It can be up to 90 characters and may appear after the headline.

You may use these fields effectively with the same perspective you use in search ads.

As the remarketing audience already visited your website, there is no point in using a general message such as "visit our website".

To achieve the best performance, you should try to provide some additional benefits or highlight some special features.

Strategies to Increase Conversion

Remarketing ads usually generate more conversion compared to display ads as they target warm audiences.

You may take some steps to increase the conversion further.

The first thing you should do is to select Topics menu and exclude irrelevant categories such as games. In addition to selecting a whole topic, you can also block irrelevant, low quality websites with negative targeting. I will elaborate on this in display ads chapter.

When deciding on the target audience, you can include the users who have visited your site up to 540 days ago. Since this is quite a long time, choices like 30, 60 or 90 days will be more appropriate.

For an ecommerce store, you should focus on the visitors who visited shopping cart page. You should create a separate ad group just for these people and increase your cost per click for this ad group.

You may test the efficiency of a message like "Thank you for visiting our website, here is 10% off discount code: ...".

The content of the remarketing message is very important.

Delivering a general message like "Browse our collection!" without an incentive to the people who have already visited your website will not produce a high conversion.

Instead of this, you should use an approach like "We are pleased that you browsed our new collection, here is a discount code to start shopping: ...".

You can determine how many times each person will see your remarketing message.

1 or 2 impressions may not be enough to get noticed and too many impressions might be annoying. You may set the daily impression limit between 5 and 8.

Should You Use Similar Target Audiences?

Based on the characteristics of the first party data lists, such as customer or remarketing lists, Google Ads creates "similar target audiences".

Similar audiences help you to expand the reach of your audiences by targeting new users having similar characteristics to your website visitors.

Google Ads system takes the existing lists and uses machine learning to understand what they have in common to find more like-minded customers.

This feature looks very attractive at the first glance as it provides you the opportunity to find new customers similar to you existing visitors, steal your competitors' visitors and reach a qualified audience. However, it may not produce high conversion if you do not use it carefully.

The Google Ads system identifies the similar audiences very broadly and gathers a large number of both relevant and irrelevant users into the same group.

For example, let's say the number of people visiting a selected category on your site is 100,000 and the number of people visiting shopping cart page is 10,000.

Based on these numbers, Google Ads system may offer you to target 1 to 5 million people as similar audiences.

You do not know the characteristics of these people and you cannot segment them.

Especially if the prices of your products are higher than your competitors, this large audience usually does not create a high conversion.

You may test the efficiency of this option by adjusting the settings of the campaign and narrowing your audience.

For search ad campaigns, you may combine similar audiences with other audience targeting options to achieve the best result.

You may target relevant affinity audiences, in-market audiences, or detailed demographics to refine the similar audiences. I will elaborate on this in the following section.

Display Ads

You can reach your audience on Google Display Network, using display ads.

Google states that, Google Display Network has over 2 million websites and reaches over 90% of people on the Internet. Your ads can appear across a large collection of websites, mobile apps, and video content.

As the remarketing system is based on people who already visited your website, this campaign type can be used to acquire new visitors.

However, since the conversion rate is notoriously low in this campaign type, you should arrange the settings of your campaign carefully.

Compared to search campaigns, display campaigns generally have lower cost per click, lower click through rate, and lower conversion.

As both the click price and conversions are low, this may yield a balanced result.

You need to adjust the campaign settings carefully to achieve a good result.

I explained the types of audiences in the "How Should You Set Up Audiences Effectively?" section.

In this section I will talk about the strategies.

Affinity Audiences

You can target affinity audiences on Google display network to reach potential customers and make them aware of your business.

Targeting the people who have demonstrated a qualified passion in a given topic is beneficial.

However, as Google targets the audience loosely and lets you to target the interest areas in general, it is better not to use this targeting alone.

In addition to selecting the affinity audience, you may use other targeting options such as demographics, location, or devices.

For search campaigns, you may achieve the best performance if you combine this targeting with other targeting options to refine the audience.

For example, regarding a financial product such as auto loans, you may select Banking & Finance category.

As this category is obviously too broad, in addition to this targeting you may select in-market > financial services > credit > auto loans to target the users who are actively in the market.

You may select 35+ men, and exclude the users in the lower 50% segment of household income.

You will achieve significantly more conversion compared to only targeting "auto loans" keyword and targeting everyone in the entire country.

For another brand, you may select Shoppers category in affinity audiences and select Luxury Shoppers subcategory.

You may combine this audience with relevant category of in-market audiences such as apparel > shoes > dress shoes to refine your target audience.

You may select 35+ men, and target business districts during working hours.

You may also combine Luxury Shoppers subcategory with your remarketing list to refine and target your website visitors.

In-market Audiences

These audiences are designed for advertisers focused on getting conversions from likely buyers.

Result-oriented businesses such as ecommerce stores may give priority to these audiences.

As these people are actively looking for a certain product or service to buy, you do not need to deal with the early stages of the shopping journey.

Instead of this, you can focus on your sales message, emphasizing discounts and comparative advantages.

You may boost your results if you refine this audience using other targeting options such as demographics, location, or devices.

For search campaigns, it is a good idea to combine this targeting with other targeting options to refine the audience.

For example, you may combine an in-market segment such as home & garden > pet supplies > cat food with similar audiences, when you are targeting "cat food" keyword.

Using remarketing you already target your own visitors. Using this targeting you may effectively reach similar audiences who are in the market to buy cat food.

This will enable you to reach and communicate with potential customers. With a tailored message, you can achieve high conversion.

If you provide SEO services, you may select business services > advertising & marketing services > SEO & SEM services.

You may combine real estate > residential properties > for sale segment with detailed demographics > homeownership status > renters to provide them a tailored marketing message. You may select 35+ married people and exclude the users in the lower 50% segment of household income.

Detailed Demographics

Detailed demographics option enables you to refine your audience by selecting parental status, marital status, education, and homeownership status.

This will help you to achieve higher conversion, especially when you combine these segments in search campaigns.

For example, if you are selling toys, you may use tailored messages by selecting segments such as parents of infants (0-1 years) or parents of toddlers (1-3 years).

You may combine this with in-market > toys segment to target people who are already in the market to buy.

You may combine in-market > computers & peripherals > computers segment with education > current college students and use tailored messages to match their perspective.

Manually Select Placements

Selecting audience targeting options is not your only alternative.

You can also manually select the websites in Google Display Network.

After selecting Placements from the menu, you can write a keyword or a site name, and the Google Ads system will list relevant placements.

It is a good idea to look at the websites where your remarketing ads are displayed.

In this way, you can see the sites your target audience visits, and the sites providing good conversion.

You may focus on those sites.

SHOPPING ADS

Google Shopping Ad campaigns enable the advertisers to directly present their relevant products to internet users.

As this campaign type targets the people who are towards the end of their shopping journey and actively looking to buy a product, they are very result oriented.

Initially this type of campaign was only available on the Google search results page. When a user was searching for a product on Google, Google was presenting relevant shopping ads.

Especially after the introduction of smart shopping campaigns, the advertisers are no longer restricted to search results pages.

Google understands the intention of the user and presents shopping ads on Google Display Network in addition to search results pages.

As this type of smart campaign also (in a way) works like dynamic remarketing campaign, it usually generates high conversion.

For this type of campaign to work Google Ads system needs to get information about your products. You must have a Google Merchant Center account to provide this information.

Google Merchant Center

Google Merchant Center is a platform where you present your product information to Google.

Google Shopping campaigns use this information instead of keywords to decide how and where to show your ads.

Google Merchant Center is completely free to use.

It acts as a base platform where you can store and organize information which you can use in shopping ads.

As you will link your Google Merchant Center account to your Google Ads account, it is a good idea to use the same Google account to create these accounts.

How does the system work?

In order to upload your product data in Google Merchant Center, you will first need to create a product feed file.

Google Ads system recognizes Text (spreadsheet) or XML file formats. Especially XML format is used widely.

You may use some plugins or extensions in ecommerce platforms to automatically generate this file.

If you cannot prepare these formats, you may need the help of a software specialist.

Google system analyzes the product information and if the product data in your primary feed meets product data specification and policies, it verifies the feed. Once it is verified, you may use the feed actively in your shopping campaigns.

How are the products updated?

The easiest way to update product information is to make your XML feed available as an URL on your website.

Google system automatically checks the newest version of the feed file from this URL and updates product information. Once you set the system correctly it will work smoothly.

You can also manually update your feed and then upload it to the platform, but this will be significantly less efficient than the automatic mechanism.

Keep in mind that it is important to keep the product feed up to date. If the information in the feed file does not match the information on your website, in other words if the users see different information on your website, Google may suspend or ban your account.

As the shopping campaigns are country-specific, you will need a separate product data feed for each target country.

In order for the feed file to provide the best result, all the fields in the XML file, especially the product names and product description fields should be well structured and should contain keywords.

The ID section is the unique identifier for a product. It is usually codes or numbers to identify the product.

The title section is the name of the product. This section is important both to get more clicks and for the Google algorithm to better match the product with the search queries.

The description section is not visible in the small tile ad format on Google search results page. When people click on the product in Google Shopping, they will see more information including the description. You should try to provide valuable information about your product.

The availability section indicates if the product is available for purchase or not.

Google accepts only three terms in this section: in stock, out of stock and preorder. You should use in stock option for the products you are actively selling on your website.

You may only use numbers in the price section of the XML file. Google will use the currency based on the country.

In the link section, you should provide the URL of the relevant product page on your website.

In the image link section, you should provide the URL of the relevant product image.

Shopping Ads

Shopping ads enable you to display your products directly on Google search results page, as well as Google shopping tab, Google search partner websites, or Google display network.

Your Shopping ads can appear at the same time as text ads on Google search results page, so you can have two spots.

The ad will consist of product title, image, and price.

When a user performs a search for a keyword such as "black dress", Google will display relevant shopping ads. This user may click on the ad to see the details or go to that product's page on your website.

As Shopping Ads are placed on top of the Google search results page, they occupy a pretty valuable area.

Search ads and the organic results are pushed below, and shopping ads usually get the attention of the searchers.

This structure leads to more clicks and sales, and it is no surprise that the retailers are moving ad budgets from search ads to shopping ads.

To publish shopping ads, you need to create a Google Merchant Center account. I explained this in the previous section.

After adding your product information using a feed file, you will need to link it with your Google Ads account.

As the users directly see product title, image, and price without clicking on the ad, these three elements highly affect the click through rate.

If the product is a standard, boxed product such as a mobile phone which is also available on other ecommerce stores, the price will be crucial for success. As the price changes often based on discounts and campaigns, you should make sure that price is accurate for every product.

The quality of the images plays an important role in non-standard products, such as dresses. The images should be appealing to achieve a high click through rate. As the images in the shopping ads are displayed as thumbnail images, your products should be clearly visible even in small images.

The product titles should be descriptive and should contain keywords to achieve the best result. You should avoid using the product names as "Dress 23082", "Dress 23083". This will significantly deteriorate your performance. You should use the names in detail such as "Sweetheart Neckline Satin Black Dress".

This will both help Google to match the product better with the search queries, and increase click through rate because the searchers will see exactly what they are looking for.

As you have the control over your XML feed file, you may exclude certain products, or in your Google Ads panel you may adjust your bidding to promote certain categories.

Shopping ads target the people who are towards the end of the shopping journey. They have already decided on the product to buy, now they are searching for the best alternative. Therefore, these ads provide high conversion.

You may use these ads together with search ads. This way, you will be displaying your product and in addition you will be talking about your advantages on Google search results page.

Google Shopping Ads operate with the pay per click principle, which means you do not have to pay anything if people do not click on your ad.

To increase the efficiency of shopping ads, you can implement certain strategies.

The first thing to consider is to segment the products in your feed.

When you set up the campaign, you will be seeing one product group with the name "All products". This means that you target your entire inventory. This will limit your testing and measuring abilities.

Segmenting the products or product groups will enable you to use different approaches regarding different product groups.

You may highlight certain products or focus on profitable product groups. You may test the performance of certain products. If you do not do this, you will be targeting all of your products and this may decrease your conversion rate.

It is a good idea to target the people who have visited your website using remarketing feature.

This way, you will be targeting the people who are familiar with your brand. When they are searching for a product, they may be inclined to buy from your store.

If you want to refine this mechanism further, you can only target certain audiences such as people who visit dress pages on your website and present them relevant products using shopping ads.

You may also use your customer data and target these people when they are searching for products. This is a high-value audience who have already bought from your store, therefore you may expect high conversion rate.

You may target new visitors using similar audience. As these people are assumed to be acting like your actual visitors or customers, this may be a good way to reach to new users and acquire new customers.

Smart Shopping Ads

As the Google Ads system advances and the artificial intelligence understands the user intent better, smart campaign types begin to take over manual campaign types.

Google launched smart shopping campaign type as a more efficient alternative to standard shopping campaigns.

This campaign subtype combines standard shopping and display remarketing campaigns to promote products and business across networks.

In the standard shopping campaigns, you may use manual and automated bidding.

Smart shopping campaign type uses automated bidding and ad placement to simplify campaign management, maximize conversion value, and expand reach.

In summary, the system wants you to give the control to Google.

Powered by artificial intelligence, Google Ads system will find the right people on networks and display them the right ads.

Although this lack of control may be expected to lower the conversion, this campaign type usually works well and provides high conversion for ecommerce stores.

As the Google system has the whole control, it knows which people will be more likely to generate conversion and targets these people prior to others.

This campaign type includes standard and dynamic remarketing campaign features.

In a way, it combines standard shopping and dynamic remarketing campaigns, uses automated bidding and ad placement to expand the reach and maximize the conversion.

The power of the system lies in predicting the intent of the users and determining the relevant products / ads to show them.

Smart shopping campaigns are automatically optimized to provide maximize conversion value for ads budget.

As this type of campaign usually performs better, you may consider pausing existing standard shopping and dynamic remarketing campaigns that promote the same products to the same audience.

This will help you to clearly monitor the performance of this campaign type.

As the system usually requires some time to learn the behavior of the users, you may need one to three weeks to see stable returns.

Dynamic Remarketing Ads

Dynamic remarketing ads enable you to show your visitors the products they browsed on your site, instead of banners.

The people who browsed the products on your site, will see these products as an ad on other sites.

As these people are interested in these products and think of buying them, they may buy them eventually after seeing them continuously.

In this regard, this ad model usually generates good sales conversion for ecommerce stores.

An article on emarketer stated that 58% of people notice retargeted ads on other websites, for products they looked up on a website.[41] 50% of people said they had gone to two or more websites before making the purchase. These numbers show the potential of dynamic remarketing ads.

The highest conversion occurs when the discount starts. When the users see the lower prices of the products that they are interested in, they are more inclined to buy them.

You may arrange the settings similar to the standard remarketing campaigns and consider the following strategies to improve your conversion.

You should focus on the users who visited shopping cart page. This should be a separate segment, you should bid high cost per click, and make sure that these people see your ads. The timing changes from person to person but you may use these ads heavily in the first one or two weeks.

It is also a good idea to target high value customers. On your Analytics panel, you can see valuable information such as age, gender and location of the users who generate high revenue. You can focus on these people.

Just like standard remarketing, Google Ads system offers responsive ad format which adjusts itself to all ad slots.

In this format, Google chooses and displays a format which it deems appropriate.

As an advertiser, unfortunately, you cannot test successful and unsuccessful formats and you are not allowed to see which of the automatically generated ad formats generate conversion.

Another important issue is that, within the responsive ad format, there is an ad format which does not show any products. This is against the mentality of dynamic remarketing perspective.

---

[41] https://www.emarketer.com/Article/Online-Buyers-Notice-Retargeted-Ads/1010122

In a way, this type of campaign now includes standard remarketing campaigns. It displays your remarketing message as well as your products.

The aim of dynamic remarketing campaigns is to increase sales by focusing on the products.

As smart shopping campaigns now include dynamic remarketing campaign features, you may give priority to smart shopping campaigns.

They usually generate better conversion compared to dynamic remarketing campaigns.

OTHER GOOGLE AD TYPES

Gmail Ads

You can target your audience when they are using Gmail.

Using Gmail ads, you can display your messages as sponsored emails in a user's inbox. In other words, this ad type functions as if you send an email to targeted users.

Ads are displayed on top of the promotion and social sections in Gmail, resembling other emails. Google ads system presents a small "Ad" tag on these ad messages.

When users click on one of these ads, it may expand just like an email. The expanded ad can include images, video, or embedded forms.

How Does It Work?

A Gmail ad is displayed first in collapsed form.

When someone clicks on the ad, it would either launch an advertiser's landing page or expand to the size of an email. The user will see the ad image and ad content.

If the user reads your message as an email and clicks on it one more time, then he/she is directed to your website.

Since this double-click structure has a negative effect on conversion rate, this ad model may be preferred with the aim of creating awareness.

As people regularly check their emails throughout the day, they may notice your message.

To create Gmail ads, you may select the campaign type as "display ads", then select "Gmail ads" in the secondary menu.

How Can You Structure Your Ad to Achieve High Conversion?

Similar to other Google Ads campaigns, high click through rate will increase your ad efficiency and improve your quality score in Gmail ads.

Gmail displays only the sender's name and the subject line of the emails in the inbox.

This means that before clicking your ad, all people see is your brand name and your headline (used as the subject of the email). You have these two fields to motivate people to click.

There is little flexibility regarding brand name. You should use your brand or company name.

If people know your brand and have a positive attitude towards your company, this will positively affect the click through rate of your ads.

For this reason, Gmail ads works better when you target audiences who are familiar with your brand.

Other than your brand name, subject line of the email (headline of the ad) remains as the only section to make the difference.

Therefore, using an effective headline is very important to motivate the target audience.

You have 25 characters to create this effect. You should communicate a clear message using up to 5-6 words, attract people's interest and motivate them to click on your ad.

As people will see your ad as an email, you should write your headline looking like the subject line of an email.

You should provide value and focus on motivating people to click.

You may consider using emojis if it is appropriate, such as pizza emoji for pizza promotion.

Best Targeting Strategies for Maximum Conversion

In order to achieve the highest conversion, you should communicate with the right people, and provide them the right message.

You can do this by segmenting and refining your audience.

You can use demographic, audience, and location targeting. You can also target specific devices to further refine your audience.

For example, when promoting a real estate project, you may target users having high household income, above a certain age, using specific mobile devices such as iPhone 11. You may then use different ad copies for men and women.

You may use keyword targeting to show your ads to users who have searched for or expressed interest in certain search phrases related to your products or services.

An exciting perspective of this keyword targeting is to use the names of competitor brands or URL addresses of their websites as keywords and target the people your competitors send email newsletters to.

Company executives love this idea. The email lists of competitor ecommerce stores, hotels and brands are very valuable. You can benefit from this.

If you have their permission, you may create special target audiences using the email addresses of your own customers or website members.

You may use Gmail ads as an alternative or in addition to your email newsletter campaigns.

Targeting your remarketing audiences using Gmail ads is also a good strategy to create high conversion.

As these people are familiar with your brand, they are more likely to click on your ad (email) and complete a conversion on your website.

You may test the performance of similar audiences to reach new people.

Gmail ad campaigns seem to have great potential, but conversion rate is usually weak in this campaign type.

For this reason, it is important to target segments carefully and monitor the results closely.

YouTube Ads

YouTube is usually perceived as a site where people spend their leisure time and it generally generates weak conversion for result-oriented websites such as ecommerce stores.

Therefore, YouTube ads may be used with the purpose of creating awareness and they may be appropriate for specific brands more than others.

For example, this campaign type may not produce high conversion for ecommerce stores, but it may be a good alternative to promote the video of a new movie or a TV commercial.

Ad Formats

You can use six types of YouTube ads.

Display Ads appear to the right of the feature video and above the video suggestions list. For larger players, this ad may appear below the player.

Semi-transparent Overlay Ads appear on the lower 20% portion of the video.

Skippable Video Ads allow viewers to skip ads after 5 seconds. Inserted before, during, or after the main video.

The problem with overlay and skippable in-stream ads is that, as the main purpose of the YouTube user is to watch videos, he or she will try to skip these ads.

A study found that 90% of people skip pre-roll ads appearing ahead of online video content.[42]

Keep in mind that many users will probably click on your ad accidentally when trying to skip the ad.

---

[42] https://www.mediapost.com/publications/article/277564/survey-finds-90-of-people-skip-pre-roll-video-ads.html

Non-skippable Ads may be an alternative to overcome this issue.

Non-skippable Video Ads must be watched before the video can be viewed. These ads can be up to 15-20 seconds long (depending on where the viewer is based).

Bumper Ads are non-skippable video ads of up to 6 seconds that must be watched before the video can be viewed.

Sponsored Cards display content that may be relevant to your video, such as products featured in the video.

One of the newest advertising formats is YouTube Shopping Video Ads. This format makes the video ads interactive by connecting viewers directly to products.

As these ads have shopping feature, they use your Merchant Center product data to generate shopping cards. You can filter your inventory or select specific products to limit which products can show with your video ads.

Strategies

To achieve the best performance, you should give importance to audience segmentation, focus on specific audiences, or publish your ads only on selected channels.

It is true that most of the people are spending their free time on YouTube, looking for entertainment. However, you should also consider that there are people watching product review or comparison videos, trying to get information about a certain topic.

You should carefully set your campaign parameters and identify your audience to achieve the best result.

You may target certain channels or videos on YouTube, by adding them in the placements section of the ad group.

You may perform a search on YouTube and list the popular videos or channels your audience likes to watch.

For example, if you have an eBook about SEO, you might target SEO tutorial channels, and present your message to people who want to learn SEO.

You may target specific keywords to communicate with the people performing relevant searches on YouTube. Similar to Gmail ads, you may use the names of competitor brands to communicate with their audience.

Using remarketing audiences is also an effective option. As these people are familiar with your brand and products, they will be more result oriented than cold audiences.

In addition to your website visitors, you may also target your customers or website members. This will be a high value group.

If you manage campaign for a fashion brand, you may display new season videos, new products, or current promotions. If your objective is to create awareness, you may consider targeting similar audiences.

Local Search Ads

People search for local businesses on Google.

Google says that there are 5 billion searches on Google for restaurants, 3 billion searches for hotels, 1 billion searches for clothing stores, 600 million searches for hair and beauty salons, and 5 million searches for coffee shops every month.

The important aspect is that these local searches turn into action.

Closeness of a location usually plays an important role in customer decision, depending on the nature of the business.

Google says 76% of people who search on their smartphones for something nearby visit a business within a day.[43]

---

[43] https://www.thinkwithgoogle.com/consumer-insights/mobile-search-trends-consumers-to-stores/

An article on Think with Google states that "near me" mobile searches that contain a variant of "can I buy" or "to buy" have grown over 500% over the last two years.[44]

This shows the potential to emphasize the location.

If you are a local business, using local search ads and optimizing your brand in Google My Business becomes inevitable.

Google My Business is a free platform provided by Google. In order to qualify for this platform, you should have a brick-and-mortar location where you interact with the customers.

As this information is visible on Google search results page and Google Maps, people see it before they come to your website (and sometimes they even do not need to come to your website).

Optimizing for this platform is inevitable, but to achieve the maximum result you should also use local search ads.

You should link your Google My Business account with Google Ads account. When accounts are linked, your locations can be used as location extensions in Google Ads.

Ads on Google can feature your business locations and lead users to call or visit your locations.

When people search for nearby businesses on Google.com or Google Maps (for example, "coffee near me"), they may see local search ads that feature relevant business locations.

You should activate location extensions to use local search ads.

Call extensions are not eligible to show with local search ad formats.

When mobile users search for nearby businesses on Google, your business location may be featured on top of the local results.

---

[44] https://www.thinkwithgoogle.com/marketing-strategies/app-and-mobile/near-me-searches/

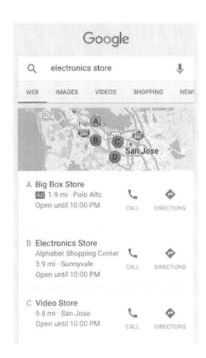

When desktop users search for nearby business on Google and click on "More places" in the local results, your business location may be featured on top of these local results.

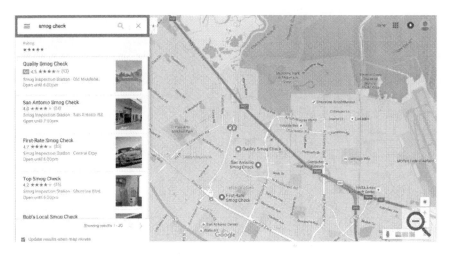

To publish ads on Google Maps, you should enable location extensions, have Google My Business listing, use location targeting and bid by location, and optimize your keywords.

Selecting the location is important in local search ads. You should consider your service area and adjust the location accordingly.

It is a good idea to bid on the names of competitor businesses to communicate with their audience.

For example, if you manage the campaign for a restaurant, you may use the names of other restaurants in the area as keywords.

TIPS TO IMPROVE CAMPAIGN PERFORMANCE

Disclaimer:

In this chapter I will provide some tips to improve campaign performance for certain cases.

I am providing these tips only to expand your perspective and give you an idea.

Every tip might not fit every campaign or may create different results in different campaigns.

You may get inspiration from these tips, determine your own strategy, and implement what will be best for your campaigns.

Case 1

Your daily budget is running out too fast.

You may consider the following tips:

- Decrease your mobile click bid by 20% to 40%.
- If you are using an automated bidding option, consider switching to manual CPC or setting a limit for CPC level.
- Use ad scheduling, pause your ads at times when you have low sales.
- Only focus on selected cities or regions, where demand for your product is high.
- By using the demographic targeting, select your target audience or exclude the segments that do not fully match with your target audience.
- Monitor the ad groups in campaigns to determine which ad groups consume your budget. Consider pausing them especially if the conversion is also low.
- For search ads, target only Google search results pages (exclude search network and display network).
- For search ads, focus on result-oriented keywords. Consider pausing generic keywords, make sure that you are using an effective negative keywords list.
- For display ads, try to narrow your audience, focusing on result-oriented segments.

Note: If you perform all of these at once, then this may significantly decrease your ad impressions. You may adopt a step by step approach.

Case 2

Your conversion is too low.

You may consider the following tips:

- You are probably targeting a wide audience. For search ads, try to combine audiences to form smaller but result-oriented segments.
- For search ads, target only Google search results pages. Focus on result-oriented keywords, consider pausing generic keywords, use an effective negative keywords list.
- If your products are expensive, select certain devices such as iPhone 11 in order to reach to a high-income audience. Select only high-income districts in selected cities.
- By using demographic targeting, select your target audience or exclude the segments that do not fully match with your target audience.
- Only focus on selected cities or regions, where demand for your product is high.
- Focus on your branded ads. Make sure you get the most from this campaign type.
- Use remarketing or customer lists to communicate with warm audiences effectively.
- Try using maximize conversions or maximize conversion value bidding options.
- Provide discounts and benefits, especially for the first-time buyers.
- Monitor the performance of ads campaigns and other channels on your Analytics dashboard. If your overall conversion is also low and you observe high bounce rates, you need to work on your website. Create landing pages for each audience, use high quality content, highlight conversion points, increase website usability.

Case 3

You want to reach new audiences.

You may consider the following tips:

- Create new campaigns to observe the performance of new audiences, such as different age groups or the people living in different locations.
- Use similar audiences. Give priority to niche segments such as similar audience of people who visit your shopping cart page. The performance will be better compared to targeting similar audience of all of your website visitors. For search ads, combine similar audiences with relevant in-market audiences to increase performance.
- Use display network targeting options to reach new audiences.
- In your existing campaigns target audiences using "observation" option. This will enable you to observe the performance of these new audiences. Use this data to target new audiences.
- Exclude remarketing audiences and customer lists in these campaigns.
- As you will start a new communication with these people, focus on introducing your brand and building trust, then talk about your comparative advantages. Make the first step easy, provide a benefit if possible.

Case 4

You want to reach global audiences.

You may consider the following tips:
- As your budget will be consumed faster, select specific audiences. Test the performance of certain countries, cities, or group of people in these countries.
- If your website is only in English, do not target any other language.
- The ad content should be in the same language as your page content.
- Focus on introducing your brand and building trust. Talk about global delivery feature, free returns, number of global customers, successful shipments, etc.
- If available, try to use location and phone extensions to build trust.
- Use negative keywords list to exclude people who are looking for local stores.
- Test the performance of in-market segments in target countries. For search campaigns combine them with other audiences to achieve a better performance.
- Most of these people will not buy immediately. Try to convince them using remarketing ads.

GOOGLE ADS CHECKLIST

Google Ads Project

1. Have you determined the KPI's to follow?
2. Have you identified the products and product categories?
3. Have you identified your target audiences?
4. Have you prepared landing pages on your website?
5. Have you decided on the campaign structure and ad groups?

Main Components of Google Ads Campaigns

6. Have you selected the location?
7. Have you specified demographic targeting?
8. Have you decided on the devices?
9. Have you selected the language?
10. Have you decided on the ad schedule?
11. Have you determined the budget and set the bidding options?

Google Search Ads

12. Have you decided on the networks?
13. Have you identified the target keywords correctly?
14. Have you prepared a negative keywords list?
15. Have you performed the necessary work to achieve a high quality score?
16. Is your ad content motivating and result oriented?
17. Are you using the appropriate ad extensions?

18. Are you using combined audiences?
19. Are you using branded, product, and dynamic search campaigns?
20. Do you monitor the performance of the keywords?

Google Display Ads

21. Are you targeting segmented audiences using remarketing campaigns?
22. Have you tested the performance of similar audiences?
23. Have you formulated strategies regarding affinity and in-market audiences?

Shopping & Other Campaigns

24. Have you created your Merchant Center account? Have you tested the performance of shopping, smart shopping, and dynamic remarketing campaigns? (for ecommerce stores)
25. Have you formulated strategies regarding Gmail ads?
26. Have you formulated strategies regarding YouTube ads?
27. Have you formulated strategies regarding Local search ads?
28. Are your using audiences effectively to refine your audience?

Other

29. Do you constantly monitor your performance and work to improve your results?
30. Google Ads is a dynamic topic. Do you follow the developments in this field closely and reflect them in your campaigns?

IT IS YOUR TURN

In this book, I explained what you need to do to achieve success in your Google Ads project.

Now it is your turn.

The first thing you need to do is to act with the perspective of conversion.

You should prepare your plan and determine KPI's to measure performance.

Implementing the strategies I provided in the relevant chapters, you should begin working on your project.

The first thing you need to do is to determine which products and services you will work on.

You should separately target each product and service having a different target audience. This will enable you to communicate with each segment using tailored messages.

You should identify your target audiences using demographic, psychographic, geographical, and behavioral segmentation.

You should prepare landing pages on your website for each target segment.

You should carefully plan your campaign structure, determine budget, and select the right bidding strategy.

You should focus on location, demographics, devices, language, ad schedule to achieve high conversion.

Selecting the right keywords increases conversion significantly in Google search ads.

You should use an effective negative keywords list, monitor the conversion of target keywords closely and arrange your budget accordingly.

You should organize your ad content effectively and use appropriate ad extensions to get the best result.

Getting high quality score is important. You should focus on click through rate, relevance, and landing page experience.

You should give importance to branded campaigns. If your website has rich content you may benefit from dynamic search ads.

You should be careful when you are working on display ad campaigns.

Most of the automated targeting options will target a wide audience and consume the budget quickly without generating conversion.

To achieve the best performance, you should arrange these settings carefully.

Remarketing ad campaigns usually generate higher conversion as they target warm audiences.

You may use similar audiences to reach new audiences. For search campaign campaigns, it is a good idea to combine these audiences with in-market audiences to increase conversion.

You may also benefit from Display ads, Gmail ads, YouTube ads, and Local search ads. but you need to target the audiences correctly.

If you are managing the campaigns for an ecommerce store, smart shopping, standard shopping, and dynamic remarketing ad campaigns will help you to increase your sales.

As Google Ads provides a very dynamic platform, campaigns need constant attention.

You should monitor the performance of your campaigns closely and make revisions if necessary.

Many brands have already implemented the strategies I have explained in this book and achieved success.

With elaborate work, you can also achieve this.

Thank you for your interest in this book.

Google Ads is a very dynamic topic and
the rules for success change constantly.

This is October 2020 edition.

From now on, you may follow the
recent developments on my website.

korayodabasi.com/digital-ads/

Feel free to contact me regarding your questions.

koray@korayodabasi.com

Manufactured by Amazon.ca
Bolton, ON